March, 1992

# Divided We Fall

# Divided We Fall

*Moving from*
*Suspicion to Solidarity*

## T. Richard Snyder

Westminster/John Knox Press
*Louisville, Kentucky*

© 1992 T. Richard Snyder
Questions for reflection and further discussion at the end of each
chapter © 1992 Westminster/John Knox Press

*Book design by Christine Leonard Raquepaw*

*First edition*

Published by Westminster/John Knox Press
Louisville, Kentucky

This book is printed on acid-free paper that meets the American
National Standards Institute Z39.48 standard. ∞

PRINTED IN THE UNITED STATES OF AMERICA

9   8   7   6   5   4   3   2   1

**Library of Congress Cataloging-in-Publication Data**

Snyder, T. Richard, 1936–
   Divided we fall : moving from suspicion to solidarity / T. Richard
Snyder. — 1st ed.
         p.      cm.
   Includes bibliographical references.
   ISBN 0-664-25297-4
   1. Liberation theology.   2. Solidarity—Religious aspects—
Christianity.   3. Ecumenical movement.   4. Theology—20th century.
5. Snyder, T. Richard, 1936–      I. Title.
BT83.57.S69 1992
230'.046—dc20                                          91-33442

to
Sergio Torres
priest and prophet

# Contents

# Foreword

This is the real T. Richard Snyder. He is one of a handful of white men I have known who feel deeply the shame of white racism and sexism, the ambiguities of all human relationships and particularly of interracial contacts, and the paradoxes of white Christianity in Western societies, yet are not so paralyzed by their guilt or calloused by failed efforts at reconciliation that they are unable to sustain an honest, reciprocal relationship with a person of another race, class, or gender.

Since the 1960s too many of us who teach in the universities and seminaries have taken a double flip and have become strangely conservative. Many have disappeared into the bowers of academe and have become indifferent and even cynical about the possibility of combining the vocation of a scholar with that of a Christian activist—of any useful collaboration between theology and the social sciences in the quest for justice and the liberation of people. Dick opens himself up to close examination. He bares his soul. If there is anything in this book that makes me slightly uncomfortable it is his wistfulness that sometimes comes across as agony because he cannot get out of his own skin and culture and become black, or Hispanic, or poor, or a woman. My experience has been that you have to look out when white Christians tell you how much they envy your closeness to the nitty-gritty of life, how much they yearn to be purified by the fires of your oppression and struggle. That's when you are about to be either patronized and blinded, taken over in a power play, or blandly exploited "in the precious name of Jesus."

But Snyder, throughout this book, wisely leaves himself room to disengage from anything that might seem to be simplistic or condescending. And in one section he clearly identifies the dangers of such wistfulness. Throughout he wrestles with two seemingly antithetical dimensions that actually cohere in the definition of his central paradigm: the individual and the communal, authentic pluralism and self-determining separatism, the spiritual and the material, the personal and political, friendship and structural alliances, the ideological and the scientific. And at the end he refuses to deny his own roots and heritage by examining the gifts that he believes Euro-American males bring to the table of solidarity with the wretched and marginalized of the earth.

I can say, with a fair degree of certainty, that much of this book comes out of three crucibles which shared in the shaping of T. Richard Snyder as a liberation theologian and ethicist: the experience of teaching at New York Theological Seminary—of being burned and healed by the passion and intensity of black and Hispanic religion as they are found in the ghettos and barrios of metropolitan New York; the experience of observing and briefly participating in the struggle in Latin America; and the experience of trying to discover a voice and praxis for white Christians engaged with nonwhite, feminist, and Third World Christians in Theology in the Americas (TIA). TIA was the intercaucus collective of progressive Christians and other activists who tried to develop a North American liberation theology during the 1970s. It was partly replicated and politicized by Jesse Jackson's Rainbow Coalition in the 1980s and on the international level today by what is called the Ecumenical Association of Third World Theologians (EATWOT).

From these three experiences Dick learned, both by observation and logical deduction, something that most North American white theologians and ethicists have either not yet learned or are not honest enough to acknowledge without falling back into the old dominating patterns: "If we who are attempting to be in solidarity in the struggle for liberation fail to claim aspects of our heritage that could be helpful in the struggle, we do a disservice to all those with whom we wish to be in solidarity" (p. 146).

The question this poses for me is: What should be the response to this book of those of us who have been the generative proponents and polemicists of the most challenging liberation theologies in North America—namely black men, black women and white women? If honest and chastened white men and women come to us bringing their own agonies, questions, gifts, and commitments—what shall we do? Of course, I am not so naive to believe for one moment that all of our problems would be solved if we should suddenly cease worshiping, meeting, planning, and acting by ourselves and unite with those who were formerly on the side of the oppressors. I know that Dick Snyder doesn't believe that either, and that is made very clear in this book. Both of us would agree with Ben Reist, who was one of the first white theologians to examine the question of solidarity and who came to it out of intergroup experiences similar to those of Snyder.

> Theologically speaking, it would be utterly fallacious to suggest that if oppressors realized they have something to gain from liberation, oppression would *ipso facto* disappear. Oppression does not ever automatically disappear. King's warnings and Cone's polemics demonstrate that once and for all. To tame them in the name of a fallacious hope is to fail to recognize that we are looking toward a promised land we have not yet entered. The point is that we are standing with them in so scanning the horizon, and we can discern the beckoning signals only with the clues they give us.[1]

---

[1]Benjamin A. Reist. *Theology in Red, White, and Black* (Philadelphia: Westminster Press, 1975), pp. 97–98.

This book is a plea that we stand together and scan the horizon with hope. More. That we walk together into the future without illusions about how easy it is to become the One, Holy, Catholic, and Apostolic Church we seek, but also without illusions about how capably we can accomplish its mission in the world without the friendship, alliances, support, and criticism of those who would march in the same direction. This is a welcome message to me and others who have labored hard over the last two decades to recover our past, our stolen legacy, and to name ourselves rather than be named—and thereby determined—by others, no matter how well-meaning and considerate. We can no longer afford to wait for a more propitious time. Our enemies are too well organized and too ruthless to be permitted any longer to keep us apart. We must listen to the appeal that Dick Snyder is making in this book if the historical project that liberation theology presumes to represent is to be a faithful and effective prescription for the sickness of this world at the turn of the twentieth century. Black and white, Hispanic, Native, and Asian American—in company with brothers and sisters overseas whose sufferings and aspirations we share—we will have to realize not only that *divided we fall,* but that even if we somehow survive the unspeakable terror to which the madness of our rulers is leading us, we can never become our true selves, cannot realize our authentic humanity as persons and groups, without all those others.

GAYRAUD WILMORE
*Professor of Church History (retired),*
*Interdenominational Center*
*in Atlanta*

# Acknowledgments

The impetus for this book grew out of two opportunities to lecture on "Solidarity and Liberation," the first at New York Theological Seminary in February 1989 and the second at Yonsei University in Seoul, Korea in May 1989. These invitations forced me to think more systematically about my own experiences as a participant in several communities concerned about the liberation struggle, especially Theology in the Americas, Witness for Peace, and New York Theological Seminary. The following fall I was granted a sabbatical that provided the time to complete a first full draft of this work. For these invitations and the sabbatical I am deeply appreciative.

I also wish to thank several colleagues who read the manuscript and made important suggestions, corrections, and challenges that have found their way into the final work: Robert McAfee Brown, Norman Gottwald, Joe Holland, Joy James, Letty Russell, Harold Dean Trulear, and William Weisenbach. They will quickly recognize those points at which I failed to heed their advice, but I trust that they also recognize the contributions they have made. Thanks also to Michael Brewer, pastor of Crescent Springs Presbyterian Church, Crescent Springs, Kentucky, for his extraordinarily sensitive and helpful questions for reflection and discussion.

I am grateful to Carole, my wife, for her painstaking editorial assistance. Whatever unclarity or verbosity still exists does so over her strenuous objections and despite her stylistic Occam's Razor.

Finally, I should like to thank whoever invented the computer. It has transformed the mechanics of writing from excruciating to merely painful.

# Introduction

We have a problem. No, it is much more than a problem, it is a tragedy of enormous proportion. Despite our prayers and marches, our preaching and lobbying, our voting and writing, our boycotts and civil disobedience, it seems that things have not changed very much. Once in a while we enjoy a small victory. But, despite all our efforts and the efforts of those who have gone before us, the world remains mired in death. Malnutrition, pollution, wars, fascism, and preventable diseases take the lives of millions annually and increasingly threaten the lives of countless others. The gap between rich and poor, within the United States and throughout the world, grows greater each year. And our great "melting pot" seems on the brink of a meltdown.

It is difficult to sustain the struggle for social transformation when we see so little success and the odds seem so stacked against us. Many have grown tired and given up. Former activists have retreated into an obsession with personal growth or succumbed to the lure of affluence. Others have found that the fires of passion have been dampened as they've taken out mortgages and college loans for their children. Even many of the victims of oppression have turned from resistance and protest to self-destruction through drugs and crime. Despair about fundamental change is rampant. Burnout is common among those who have tried to hang in there and not give up hope. But the troops are so few and the task is so enormous that those remaining have all they can do to keep their heads above water. If this were not enough, many of the persons and organizations that have continued to work on the issues are as deeply divided as the larger society they are seeking to change.

Increasingly, I have become convinced that divisions among those who seek justice are at the heart of the failure to achieve fundamental social change. The forces of death and destruction are too strong to yield to anything but unified resistance. How can we prevail against such overwhelming odds if we who seek transformation remain divided?

In the vanguard of this problem is the church. We profess to be "one in Christ," yet we are separated at every level. Sunday morning at 11:00 remains the most segregated hour of the week. Mistrust abounds in congregations and denominations alike. Ecumenicity—the great hope of the fifties and sixties—is in retreat. Stereotypes define most of our interactions, and women continue to be relegated to secondary places in the life of the church. If we cannot get even our own house in order, how can we expect to be instruments of change within the larger society? For the church to be an effective agent of transformation it must make serious strides to overcome the alienation that exists within its own ranks.

But the demand for unity does not relate only to our ability to be effective in mission. It also relates fundamentally to our identity and the authenticity of our life.

We long for the dividing walls of hostility to be torn down. We have had enough of the mistrust, the fears, the hatred, and the miscommunication bred of our divisions. And we are not alone. We are not the first generation to long for the end to our divisions. Throughout the history of the church efforts at unity have abounded. Within this century the ecumenical movement has catapulted the issue of Christian unity into the forefront of the religious agenda. The development of the World Council of Churches, along with various national and regional councils of churches throughout the world, and denominational mergers and liturgical sharing across traditional lines have reshaped the ecclesiastical landscape.

When we consider, however, the state of the church in the light of the biblical claim about our oneness, all these efforts have produced little more than a facelift. When the Dominican Republic decided to make an all-out effort to develop its tourism industry, it faced a problem. The major road leading from the airport to the city of Santo Domingo ran through several miles of squalid shacks inhabited by the desperately poor. Rather than dealing with the conditions of poverty, the government erected a series of buildings on both sides of the highway, just tall enough and deep enough to hide the teeming slums behind them. When the tourists arrived they saw only the new buildings.

Behind the formal claims and activities of the ecumenical movement is a church that is impoverished. While the motives of those involved in the construction of ecumenicity are not necessarily analogous to the builders of the Dominican Republic's "poverty screen," the results are strikingly similar. Despite appearances, our divisions remain and are sapping our lifeblood from us. We need to restore what is behind the facade for the sake of our own faithfulness and health.

This book is a response to our divisions and our failed attempts at unity. What follows is a brief sketch of the terrain we will cover as we seek to understand what it means to be one in Christ. Although I speak as a Christian about the church, that is not the limit of the book's horizon. The unity we seek is a unity of all humankind, indeed a recovery of the "uni-verse." It is a unity that seeks to overcome all divisions, not just within the church or even among religions, but among all the inhabitants of our global village. I begin with the church and our responsibility as members of that body, because that is our particularity, our home if you will. But much of what is said is offered to all groups struggling for liberation.

Our desire for unity in Christ is evidence of something deep within us—even deeper than the racism, sexism, classism, homophobia, and other evils that so deeply divide us. Our desire for unity is the image of God in us, it is the Spirit of God moving upon the waters of our chaotic world. It is a recognition of our true destiny, and we ignore it at our own peril.

But is our desire for unity also a cop-out? We are calling for unity just when so many of the victims in our society are claiming their particularity, their separateness. During the last twenty-five years African Americans, women, Latinos, gays, lesbians, and others have claimed their distinctiveness and organized separately in order to find a voice and press for justice. Is it not necessary to affirm the differences inherent among us and even to support separation, at times, along lines of race, gender, sexual orientation or classes, in order to be effective in the battle for justice as well as for the sake of sheer survival? Is the call to unity simply a last-gasp attempt on the part of those who have been in control to maintain the status quo?

Certainly when one looks at the various forms of church unity that have dominated the scene during this century there is cause for suspicion. Almost uniformly they have failed to provide us with an adequate foundation for the task before us. They have been based upon confessional agreement (getting people to affirm a certain set of basic beliefs), organizational consolidation (evident in the many mergers of denominations such as recently occurred among the Lutherans or between the southern and northern Presbyterians) or liturgical cooperation (such as the Lutherans and Episcopalians celebrating the Eucharist together). These efforts, important as they may be in their place, have served only to compound the problem. With rare exception, they have failed to change the fundamental dynamic of control within those churches and ecumenical organizations. Essentially, power continues to remain in the hands of Euro-American* males.

---

*I have chosen to use the term "Euro-American" rather than "white" for several reasons. First, it is parallel to the use of the terms Latino, Asian American and African American currently favored by many persons of color. Second, the fact is that our skin color is not white; for some of us it is closer to pink, others a swarthy tan. Third, the color white has frequently been identified in many cultures with purity. There is no need to continue to foster this delusion of the purity of the Euro-American peoples.

This history gives rise to such deep suspicions about ecumenicity that we are forced to explore new territory, to seek a new basis for our unity in Christ. It is this demand for a new interpretation that gives rise to the understanding of Christian unity as solidarity in the struggle for liberation.

Solidarity conjures up images of the Polish freedom struggle and the early labor union movement within our own country. Such a political implication is intentional. There can be no unity that does not take seriously the structural dimensions of our lives, the social arrangements that shape so much of who we are and what we do. Solidarity involves politics, economics, media, culture, and all aspects of society.

However, it is necessary to extend the meaning of solidarity beyond politics to include the more interpersonal dimensions that are implied by friendship, for if our unity is simply a strategic one we shall have failed to grasp the essential connection that God has intended for us. To be in solidarity means to be both political allies and friends. Such a direction is very much in keeping with the increasing emphasis throughout much of the church today upon the inextricable link between the spiritual and the social, the personal and the political. In the notion of Christian unity as solidarity in the struggle for liberation, these two often-separated dimensions of our lives come together.

There are many who wish to link themselves in solidarity with others in the struggle for liberation but who find it difficult, if not impossible, to do so. Despite its desires and best efforts, each group often has found itself rejected, mistrusted, and angry. The progressive movement throughout the country and within the church in the United States is deeply fractured. All our speeches about unity seem ephemeral, a promise today but invisible tomorrow. We must discover what blocks us from solidarity and the steps we can take that will lead us toward a church and a world in which we stand together as sisters and brothers.

There are no easy answers, no formulas that can be applied from elsewhere. But there are discoveries to be unfolded from our own journeys, from the journeys of those who surround us throughout our world today, and from those who have gone before us. This is no task for a straight Euro-American male who holds a privileged position within the professional world of theological education. But then, it is no task for any single individual. Whatever appropriate steps lie ahead will have to emerge from the common sharing and efforts of all who seek to be faithful to the promise of a transformed life and world. It is in this hope that I risk offering some of the hunches and convictions that have emerged out of my own journey toward solidarity.

By seeking to be in solidarity, people such as I inevitably raise suspicions and fall into traps. It is important for us and for those with whom we would be in solidarity to face squarely some of the limits and temptations of this participation so that we can move beyond naivete and good feelings toward effective action for transformation. And so we explore the role of Euro-American males in this struggle and the risks that our participation poses.

It has been stated accurately that the leadership of the liberation struggle must come from the oppressed, from those held silent and invisible by their bonds. Only those who know the tragedy of being oppressed can be trusted to lead us into a transformed world. While this is absolutely essential, the question remains whether the rest of us who would participate in liberation must watch on the sidelines or whether we have something crucial to contribute. We will conclude with an exploration of the potential contribution to liberation that might be made by those of us who have shared in the benefits of the culture of oppression but who wish to stand with the oppressed.

This is not a complete word. It cannot be, given the one who speaks it. But it is a word that grows out of a love for justice and a longing for our potential unity. Perhaps it is a word that can elicit other voices, and together we can become a word that cannot be conquered by the powers of silence.

# 1
# *The Tragedy of Our Divisions*

I n a world as tragically divided as ours, it is scandalous that the church falls so short of the vision of unity that is promised in the New Testament epistles. Our divisions fly in the face of the fundamental claim of scripture that we are one in Jesus Christ.

Paul tells the church in Corinth that the differences present among them are not to be cause for pride or superiority; rather, he says, each person is an important and necessary part of God's plan, having different functions just as different parts of the body have different functions. The bottom line is that we all have been baptized "into one body" (1 Cor. 12:13). To the church at Rome he writes that we are "one body in Christ" (Rom. 12:5). In Galatians we are told that in Jesus Christ there is "neither Jew nor Greek, there is neither slave nor free, there is neither male nor female; for you are all one in Christ Jesus" (Gal. 3:28). And in the letter to the church at Ephesus we read that the divisions between Jew and Gentile have forever been put to an end for Jesus "is our peace, who has made us both one, and has broken down the dividing wall of hostility" (Eph. 2:14).

The reality we experience is in stark contrast to those claims. We are not one. We are a church divided. Caucuses, interest groups, and old boys' networks abound. It is a rare denominational or interdenominational gathering in which mistrust and tensions between the races, genders, and even sections of the country are absent. It may not be the way we want it, but it is the way things are.

## A Threefold Tragedy

The tragedy of our divisions is multiple. First, it is against God's basic intention for us. The creation narratives point decisively to our kinship. We are created in the image of God, an image of fundamental relatedness. In fact, the doctrine of the Trinity has at its heart the inescapable relatedness of God's nature. Whether or not we can fully understand or accept this doctrine in all its metaphysical and speculative dimensions, we can see, at the very least, that to speak of God as three persons is to assert that God is eternally in relationship. It was impossible for many within the church to portray God as simply an all-sufficient, self-contained being, existing apart from all else. And so the doctrine of the Trinity speaks of God as eternally interrelated. If we are created in the image of a God who is irrevocably in relationship, then we too must be made for such oneness.

We need not involve ourselves, however, with formal doctrines to grasp the truth of this claim. The scriptures from beginning to end tell us of our essential unity. The story of Cain and Abel accurately portrays the essence of God's purpose for our lives. We are meant to be our sister and brother's keeper. (See Genesis 4.) And in the First Epistle of John, chapter four, we are told that to know God is to love one another and to hate our brother is to hate God. We are called to be lovingly related to all others. Martin Buber, a twentieth century philosopher and one of the revivers of Jewish mysticism, captured it well when he paraphrased the familiar passage in the Gospel of John, "in the beginning is the relation."[1] Anything less is a mere shadow of the powerful image of our creation in God's image. Our divisions deny the very creation.

Second, our divisions run counter to the delight of those moments when we have experienced that oneness firsthand. Most of us have known grace, forgiveness, total acceptance, and the breaking down of the hostilities. We have known what it is to be trusted by a child, though we were painfully aware of our failures. We have known the forgiveness and unquestioning welcome experienced by the prodigal son. We have been surprised by the hospitality of those we feared because of our ignorance. The overwhelming beauty and power of these experiences stands in sharp contrast to the pain of our divisions. Infrequent as they may be, they have made us restless for the fullness that has been promised. To settle for anything less, we now know, is to live a lie.

Finally, our divisions irreparably damage the possibilities for redemption in our time. From the beginning to the end of the scriptures God is portrayed as one who seeks out the lost, who cares for and tends the flock, who champions the cause of the weak, who works to create a new heaven and a new earth, and who, in the incarnation, sacrifices everything to restore us to our rightful relationships with each other, with the world, and with the source of our being. God longs to make us one, to restore us to our wholeness.

But God's redeeming activity is inextricably linked with our action and faithfulness. If the incarnation means anything, it is that God has chosen to redeem the world through human agency. Redemption is not a magical act by which God waves a wand and overcomes the alienation. Redemption is a historical process, with all the fits and starts, all the strengths and weaknesses, all the victories and defeats of our human endeavors. Redemption depends upon human response and responsibility. In the light of the incarnation we understand that our failure to live as redeemed people defeats the process of redemption.

Our divisions have weakened us in the struggle for transformation at a time when a disaster of Armageddon-like proportions is frighteningly imaginable. In fact, for some communities Armageddon is already present. Given the destructive possibilities loose in our world today, it is conceivable that conflict will not result in redemption but annihilation. Even if this apocalyptic mood is not shared by everyone, to most it is clear that the cost of maintaining our current course of racism, worldwide imperialism, patriarchy, ecological destruction, homophobia, and militarism is so enormous that we *must* find a way to be part of God's redeeming, liberating action for the sake of our planet and its people. But that will demand some form of unity.

## A Legacy of Failure

Sadly, it does not appear that we are advancing toward unity. Throughout our nation's history there have been many attempts to unite for the sake of transformation. But, repeatedly, they have disintegrated, and the promise has turned to bitter ashes. The alliance between the abolitionist and woman's suffrage movement that was so strong before the Civil War was severed after Emancipation out of fear on the part of many abolitionists that such a continued link would weaken the general population's support for Reconstruction, and because of the latent racism that lay dormant but always ready to emerge within the Euro-American community.

During the early 1900s many African Americans and Euro-Americans stood together under the banner of the labor movement. However, because many socialists sought to subsume everything under issues of economics and employment the specificity of racism was lost. Increasingly the plight of African Americans became less visible and the alliance dissolved.[2]

Under the leadership of Dr. Martin Luther King, Jr., a strong coalition began to take shape, linking racism, poverty, and imperialism. King's "poor people's campaign" and his opposition to our war in Vietnam, while generating disagreement within his own leadership ranks, pulled together people with previously disparate agendas. With his murder, the fragile unity soon unraveled.

There are numerous reasons for our current failure to unite for the sake of a transformed world. Some of the factors that

account for this fragmentation within the progressive movement in the United States and the churches are external ones
and others are internal.

Externally, Dr. King's murder removed from our midst a
charismatic visionary who had the ability to unite millions
across seemingly insurmountable boundaries. According to
sociologist and political theorist Max Weber, the early stages
of change are dependent upon the charisma of a leader or
small group. After some time, the leader's role is not so critical
because an organization develops to take over the tasks that
were at first handled by the leader and a few close followers.[3]
Dr. King's death came at a fairly early stage in the movement
to link racism, poverty, and imperialism. In fact, it was at the
time that he began to make such connections, forging a unified
challenge to the logic and power of the United States, that he
was killed. This has led some to speculate that it was precisely
the linking of these formerly divided movements that posed
such a threat and necessitated his assassination.

Another external factor that ruptured the delicate unity was
the cutback in funding granted to movements for change from
traditional sources such as foundations, churches, and individuals. A certain timidity became evident in the late sixties
and early seventies. One such case involved the United Presbyterian Church in the U.S.A. (now part of the Presbyterian
Church (U.S.A.)), the denomination in which I am ordained
and serve. The denomination had been a leader in support of
the civil rights movement, providing significant staff and program funds since 1963. In 1971 Angela Davis, an African
American university professor from California and supporter
of the Black Panthers and member of the Communist party,
was arrested in connection with the murder of a prison guard.
Many felt that she would have a difficult time obtaining a fair
trial and through the denomination's Commission on Church
and Race (COCAR) ten thousand dollars was provided toward
a legal defense fund. The same agency previously had provided similar support for others. A general furor developed
throughout the denomination, denouncing this use of church
funds. In response, twenty African American Presbyterians

gave their personal funds and repaid the grant to the church. But the furor continued, and many Euro-Americans impugned the integrity of the committee, its members, and those associated with it.[4] Pressure mounted and our denomination began a process of retrenchment from the struggle against injustice that has lasted until today. This retrenchment has meant that supporters of racial, economic, and international justice and peace have had to fight over fewer and fewer crumbs. Tragically, this story or others like it could be repeated with respect to many of the churches and foundations in our country.

Lastly, the conservative trend within our country has resulted in a national mood shift and reactionary governmental policies and priorities, further eroding the financial support for progressive movements and causing many who were on the fence to retreat from the struggle. Governmental funds for the causes of justice have almost dried up. We haven't been able to mount even a minor skirmish on poverty during the past twenty years, let alone a war on poverty. The Peace Corps is a shadow of its former self. Social programs such as Section 8 Housing have been eliminated in the face of dramatically increased homelessness. And so it goes.

But our failure is not simply attributable to external causes. Internal dynamics within many of the groups also contributed to the breakdown of unity. One was the institutional survival mentality. In the face of severe financial cutbacks more and more groups found themselves facing the possibility of extinction. This prospect led to serious competition and infighting. To justify their own existence some groups began to disparage others. Groups were forced to fight for their life, to look out for number one.

Perhaps even more important was the failure of most progressive groups to grapple seriously with the sexism within their own organizations. This gave rise to an increasing feminist consciousness that drove many women toward each other for support and away from patriarchal organizations, no matter how lofty their goals. This led to the creation of various women's organizations and projects, thereby increasing the number of groups vying for the financial crumbs that were still available.

Finally, the process of claiming distinctiveness or particularity was new for most people, and in the enthusiasm to discover and affirm their own identity and importance the delicately woven fabric of cooperation began to unravel. It was analogous to the process of individuation when an infant learns that there is a me and a not me. Such self-affirmation is an essential step in the maturation process, but it often leads to serious rejection. Many groups affirmed their distinctiveness at the expense of solidarity. Claiming a vanguard role, they insisted that their issue or constituency be the primary focus of the struggle for justice and liberation. In the absence of a unifying leader, affirmations of distinctiveness became the occasion for division. Not until Jesse Jackson's Rainbow Coalition was there a serious effort to affirm distinctiveness and unity as related.

## The Ecumenical Movement and the Failure of Unity

Just as has the larger society, the church has failed in the task of unity, all the publicity about the ecumenical movement to the contrary. None of the many efforts at unity on the part of the organized ecumenical movement has even approximated the oneness that the scriptures portray. As author James Kelly points out, we are at a point in the "spiral" of ecumenism when the bases for formal ecumenism have been crumbling, and what we have now is not true unity but toleration. The substitute for a unity born out of the power of the Christian myth is a tolerant religious pluralism born out of political necessity.[5]

The failure of the church to achieve the unity to which we have been called is rooted in the unwillingness of those who have been in control to give up power. The essential reason for this failure is that most attempts at unity have not been based on sharing power but rather on allowing those on the margins to participate only as spectators and supporters. This can be seen in the history of the modern ecumenical movement, in both its international and national manifestations. Within this history unity has taken three dominant forms: confessional agreement, organizational consolidation, and liturgical cooperation.

The World Council of Churches grew out of two different emphases that emerged during the early 1900s. These emphases gave rise to two movements: Life and Work, and Faith and Order. Both movements believed that the divisions across denominational lines had gone beyond the normal differences of expression and cultures and that these divisions thwarted the witness of the church to the world. The advocates of Life and Work thought that the church should not make confessional agreement its principal concern but rather should focus on the critical issues facing the world such as poverty, war, and injustice. The Faith and Order proponents advocated the importance of agreement about certain doctrines they considered basic, without which they felt it was impossible for true unity to exist.

Life and Work proponents argued that in beginning with doctrine and pressing for commonality of thought, unnecessary divisions were created. Since the church had been characterized by doctrinal disputes throughout its history, they felt that it would be better for Christians to get on with the task of giving a cup of cold water in Jesus' name and to let the doctrinal issues take second place.

One might accuse some of the Life and Work advocates of a certain naivete in their press for social action. It is finally impossible to avoid beliefs, analysis, theory, and doctrine. We may pretend that it is unimportant, but every action is shaped by prior understanding. To the extent that people share certain prior understandings, they may or may not be prepared to work together around a certain issue or problem. For example, the reason some of us make world peace our rallying point is that we agree about some fundamentals with respect to the vision of peace, the evils of war, permissible strategies for change, and current international relations. While we might not begin our cooperation with attempts to articulate our fundamental agreements, without them we would probably not cooperate. There is a connection between thought and action, between word and deed. A certain commonality of "confession" is essential for cooperation, however informal and unarticulated it may be. You cannot avoid doctrine.

Jacques Ellul has criticized such approaches to what he calls "service theology" as being devoid of the essentials of the gospel claims.[6] We begin, according to him, with a word, with a story, and a common confession. Though he wrote these thoughts well after the Life and Work movement, they parallel the essential critique offered by the Faith and Order movement during the early days of the debate.

In the development of the World Council of Churches, the Faith and Order approach won the day, giving shape to a very specific kind of ecumenicity. Tragically, the shape it took meant that the voices of the marginal were largely unheard, and each hearing had to be fought for against great odds.

This fatal flaw was not necessarily due to malevolence on the part of those who envisioned and led the ecumenical movement, but it flowed from an uncritical use of certain doctrines and confessions as the basis or guidelines for all discussion and thought. The problem with an approach to unity that is based on confessional agreement is that it always assumes a certain basic orthodoxy, that is, a baseline of doctrine that sets the guidelines for all further thought. Such a basic foundation of beliefs does not drop from heaven. All beliefs and doctrines are inevitably shaped by people in response to their own historical and contemporary circumstances. Doctrines or confessions always grow out of a specific, and limited, context. When these doctrines become the basic guidelines for thought and action, serious problems arise for those whose circumstances and community are different.

This is the problem that has hindered the modern ecumenical movement. Even though a variety of persons are invited to participate, they are all guided by the same thoughts. It is not that they all think the same, rather that the arbiter (i.e., the confessional guidelines) is not similarly diverse. The problem is that virtually all basic Christian doctrinal guidelines have been drawn by men—mostly Western men. Official Christian doctrine has been an intellectual form of male imperialism with few exceptions to this day. This means that doctrinal developments generated out of the experience of women, or people of color, or non-Westerners have been expected to conform to guidelines that grew out of Western male experience.

The limitations and distortions this causes are well documented by Melanie A. May in her study of the role of women in the ecumenical movement and the consistency with which women's experience and thoughts have been discredited, resulting in ostracism or token treatment.[7] Even though substantial numbers of women have been involved in the ecumenical movement (though far from proportionate), they have been limited by confessional guidelines that were foreign to the core experiences of many of them.

This may seem to be an unfair criticism of the World Council of Churches, which has been constantly and increasingly attacked by conservatives for selling out to the supporters of radical politics and Third World revolutions. But it is important to realize that the voices heard in the Committee to Combat Racism or in the Church and Society Committee are distinctly in the minority within the World Council's history. They have gained notoriety as they have been singled out for infamy. The truth is that until very recently the progressive elements of the World Council of Churches have been relatively few. The major control of decisions and money has remained in the hands of the dominant churches and their representatives. As more churches from the Third World gain a voice and influence, we are witnessing a process similar to what has happened within our cities. Those with the money who formerly controlled matters have begun to cut back, to take their money and run, leaving the marginalized in control of a sinking ship.

By attempting to build unity on the basis of commonly agreed beliefs, control has remained in the hands of the dominant group. The majority have been kept on the margins.

When unity is approached from the perspective of organizational consolidation the problem is compounded. Those who imagine, orchestrate, and implement organizational alignments are generally the power brokers of their respective organizations. When you trace the history of the World Council of Churches, the National Council of the Churches of Christ in the U.S.A. (NCC), and many denominations, you see this dynamic underscored. It was not the marginal churches or persons who were instrumental in originating the alignments, but the establishment. Only later, when power had been consolidated, were the marginal voices allowed a hearing. Then, as noted above, the tendency is for those who called the shots to withdraw.

Organizational consolidation has frequently been a move to shore up embattled organizations, all in the name of Christian unity. Most of the mergers among United States denominations have occurred because of diminishing numbers, finances, and influence. One need not be a cynic to wonder about the motivation behind the church's merger mania. While there are undoubtedly many individuals who have worked for consolidation out of a vision of genuine unity, it appears that most of the church's organizational consolidation has been done not for the sake of biblical inclusiveness and unity but for the sake of salvaging the waning power of those who have been at the top. Genuine unity does not evolve from mergers that seek to maintain control in the hands of the traditional power-wielders.

When unity is pursued along the lines of liturgical cooperation or agreement some of the same limitations are evident. It is certainly a good thing for church bodies that formerly excluded ordained clergy of other denominations from celebrating the Eucharist to have opened themselves to a broader inclusiveness, such as has occurred between the Lutherans and the Episcopalians. However, when we look for a broader inclusiveness that goes beyond the currently ordained clergy leadership, there is little movement. In most churches the laity are still not allowed to celebrate the sacraments. And in many church bodies women still are not ordained. Those who have formulated and now conduct the liturgy remain, with a few exceptions, the same controlling group. Where there is liturgical cooperation, it is based upon doctrinal guidelines established by the very people who have been in control all along—ordained males. These guidelines determine who may conduct the liturgy and under what circumstances. Because liturgy is tied in with orthodox thought and the traditional organization of power, it has been possible for many churches to resist such steps as the ordination of women. As long as Christian unity is approached as essentially a liturgical issue, there is little hope of genuine oneness.

There are exceptions to these observations, naturally. But the basic point is valid. Unity formulated on the basis of doctrinal agreement, organizational consolidation, or liturgical cooperation suffers the limitation of control and guidance by the dominant powers. These aspects of church life are not the way to unity but are the legitimate expressions of a more fundamental foundation. That is not to say that shared liturgy or confessional agreement cannot contribute to fundamental unity. They can and must be part of an overall dynamic. However, they are not the way to unity; they may contribute to it, and they certainly flow from it, but unity's essential foundation is to be found elsewhere.

Generally speaking, the unity we have forged through confessional agreement, organizational consolidation, and liturgical cooperation has not led to the oneness of which Paul spoke. At its best, it has achieved little beyond raising our awareness of the desirability of unity. At its worst, it has merely been a form of co-optation.

In the light of this history it is undeniable that there are enormous dangers inherent in the attempt to create Christian unity. Far too often the notion of unity has been advanced by those in control to calm the restlessness of the controlled. South African Christians involved in the struggle against apartheid have warned of this danger in their *Kairos Document,* "the peace that the world offered us is a unity that compromises the truth, covers over injustice and oppression and is totally motivated by selfishness."[8] Given this history we would do well to be suspicious whenever we hear anyone speak of unity.

As Juan Luis Segundo, a Latin American Roman Catholic liberation theologian, points out, it is suspicions of this nature that drive us to explore new ways of thinking about what we believe and what we practice.[9] If unity is part of God's intention, promised us in scripture, and essential for the transformation of our world, we dare not ignore the task. However, since unity has so often been a mechanism for maintaining the status quo, we dare not simply rework the old ideas and attempts. We must risk new thoughts and new actions. What does it mean to say that we are one in Jesus Christ? What does it mean in the face of the divisions that continue to exist? What does it mean in the face of the historical misuse of the claim? The tenacity of the vision will not let us go, but the historic perversions of the vision force us to a new interpretation.

I suggest that the basis for an authentic Christian unity is to be found in solidarity in the struggle for liberation. Before we can understand fully what this means, we need to explore further what it is that keeps us locked in the divisions that characterize our society and the church: divisions of power, of privilege, of access, of legitimation, based on race, gender, and class. Why is it that despite the claims of the gospel the divisions continue?

## Why The Divisions Persist

First, the divisions work for those who are in power. Having each of us at one another's throats means that we are diverted from the essential enemy. As long as African Americans and Koreans are fighting over control of a few stores on 125th Street in Harlem, they are diverted from seeing the larger economic controls that force them to fight for crumbs. This is not simply a matter of ambitious Koreans invading the turf that has been staked out by African Americans. It has a far more complicated and lengthy history having to do with the residual effects of slavery, the ongoing policies and practices of U.S. racism toward African Americans and Asians, and the basic patterns of investment, provision of goods and services, employment/unemployment, and economic control.

As long as men take out their frustrations with their work by abusing their wives or children, their rage will not be directed toward improving conditions in the workplace. Demeaning others will have no effect upon the shape of their jobs.

As long as the poor, whether Euro-American, Latino, or African American, Native American, or Asian American, whether men or women, are forced to compete for limited resources, nothing will change. The unjust zoning, investment and tax laws, and legislative apportionments that benefit the privileged and cause the scarcity of resources for the poor will remain hidden and go unchallenged.

Our divisions work to maintain the status quo. "Divide and conquer" is a recognized strategy for winning, and whether or not those in power are always intentional in its use, its effect is undeniable. Our divisions allow those in power to avoid making the necessary changes.

Second, the divisions work for many of those who are powerless. Divisions born out of oppression can sometimes be worn as badges of honor. Divisions can offer a false identity that serves as an anchor in turbulent waters. It is a way to name yourself, if only negatively, if only by default. We may have a new name written down in glory, but it is tempting to stay with what we know, identifying ourselves with a place, a pattern of behavior or a group, even though the identity may be a negative one.

We have only to witness the reluctance of many people to leave situations of oppression. Why they remain is a complicated issue, involving systemic injustice, fear of reprisal and rejection, and lack of support. In addition, some are hesitant to leave or give up their condition because, in a perverse sort of way, there is security in the familiar. Victim habits die hard. The old identities and conditions may offer a certain "comfort," and the struggles and uncertainties of creating a new future may seem overwhelming in the face of everything else. When the children of Israel found the wilderness wandering more than they had bargained for, they murmured and longed to return to the leeks and garlic of Egypt—the land of their slavery.

Third, there are mechanisms that camouflage or mystify the reality of the divisions. The myths of "the American Dream" and the "melting pot" do this. If the United States *is* a melting pot, and if there *is* a dream that is accessible to all who would dare dream it, then we are led to think that the divisions are temporary and that they exist only because of our failure to believe or strive hard enough. According to the myths, all who wish to and strive may find their way into the mainstream. When these myths are combined with a social theory that describes our divisions as merely functional differences, we are hooked.

One of the most influential sociological theories in the shaping of the American consciousness has been structural functionalism.[10] According to this theory, our society is divided into various groups, each with its appropriate function or part to play. Problems do not arise from the differences among the various groups but from each group's failure to play out its given role or function appropriately so that equilibrium can be achieved. When each group is playing its appropriate part, as in a play or in a game, the differences will not be divisive but purposeful and healthy.

Functionalist social theory has failed to acknowledge, however, that these apparently natural or normal functions for each group are determined by those in control, the traditional power-wielders. We can see this in the battle over redlining, the process by which a bank defines a certain area (draws a red line around it on a map) as undesirable for mortgages and other investments. When this occurs, we witness a struggle between relatively powerless groups—churches, tenant groups, and community organizations—and the dominant powers—banks, insurance companies, realtors, and investment firms. The bank that redlines is backed by the overall interests of capitalism that define the bank's function almost

enormous obstacles that stand in our way, not the least of which are false notions of what constitutes our unity. If unity is not to be found in the traditional approaches that have characterized the ecumenical movement of our time, then we must search for a new way. That way is to understand our oneness in terms of solidarity—solidarity in the struggle for liberation.

But before we can explore this interpretation we must try to understand the positive functions of our differences and distinctiveness. Unity cannot be reduced to uniformity. If we wish to be one, what do we make of our differences? It is that question to which we turn now.

# For Reflection

1.   Consider the creation of humanity in Genesis 1:26–27. How does our creation in the image of God suggest that we are meant for relatedness? How is our maleness/femaleness related to the image of God?
2.   The parable of the prodigal son (Luke 15:11–32) reveals God's desire to relate to us in love. What does the parable suggest about our responsibility to love each other?
3.   Can you think of moments when you have experienced acceptance and oneness with another person? What feelings were evoked in you? Which is more difficult—to accept or be accepted? Can you imagine a world in unity?
4.   We usually think of Armageddon as a catastrophic event of global proportions. What does it mean to say that "for some communities Armageddon is already present"? Can you think of a community that is presently suffering Armageddon?
5.   Is self-affirmation an unhealthy thing if it undermines cooperation? Have there been times in your life when "individuation" has caused stress and rejection?
6.   What marginal voices are not being heeded in the church

today? Make a list. For each group consider how the church might be enriched by that perspective. Why is the church so often deaf to the witness of people on the fringes?

7. How did the doctrine of the fatherhood of God grow out of a specific, historical context? What reaction might the fatherhood of God elicit from feminist Christians? Ethnic Americans? Gays and lesbians? Third World victims of colonialism? Should ancient doctrines be modified to fit changing contexts?

8. Sometimes oppressed people may derive an identity from their suffering. Is this a true identity? Have you ever defined yourself by hardship or suffering?

9. Are you troubled by the thought of a God who is limited by the constraints of history? How does the incarnation illuminate this idea?

# For Further Discussion

1. How can we reconcile Paul's claims for the unity of the church and our experience of church disunity? Do you think the early church was a unified church? Can you cite biblical evidence for your answer?

2. Would you agree that salvation means reconciliation? What is our responsibility in salvation? Can our resistance thwart the saving work of God?

3. Do you feel it was appropriate to use church funds in the legal defense of Angela Davis? Why did the Angela Davis controversy continue to rock the Presbyterian church even after the church funds were repaid from private sources?

4. Would you agree that there has been a national shift toward conservatism? What may have caused this shift? When do you think this process began? Are there signs of reversal?

5. Is internal sexism still an undermining influence in the

progressive movement? How has the mission and life of
the church been affected by sexism? Is this more apparent in congregations or in national church structures?

6.  In ecumenical relationships, what is the difference between toleration and true unity? Imagine a Presbyterian church and a Roman Catholic church as next-door neighbors. What would mutual toleration look like? True unity? What if you add a fundamentalist, charismatic congregation?

7.  Put yourself in the role of a male minister in a church that does not ordain women. From that perspective explain why women should not be ordained. Let another person, in the role of a woman called to ministry, explain why women should be ordained. How are tradition and doctrine used in church "power politics"? Is the Bible also a tool of power?

8.  What are the three traditional approaches to ecumenical unity? What is the weakness of each perspective? What progress has resulted from these approaches?

# 2
# Divisions, Differences, and Separation

If God intends for us to be one, then our divisions are a form of radical evil. To stand against one another as enemy or alien is to be out of relationship, not only with the other but also with God, the world, and ourselves. We are alienated from all that we are meant to be. These divisions are clearly rejected by scripture—they are not part of God's intent.

Does this mean that all divisions and all differences are to be rejected? Does unity imply the end of differences, distinctions, and even disagreements? Is there no place for African American theology, feminist theology, Korean *minjung* theology, or Hispanic theology? Are the differences between sacramentalists and free church, episcopal and congregational forms of government, and the host of other expressions of our faith that distinguish us one from another to be done away with?

## A Biblical Paradigm for Dealing with Differences

The answer to these questions is rooted in the same texts on unity with which we began chapter 1. It is quite evident that, despite the claim that there is neither male nor female in

Christ, there continue to be men and women in the church. Only the most fertile imagination could lead to an interpretation of this text as a promise of the collapsing of sexual differentiation into an androgynous amalgam. The issue was not the elimination of gender differences but the elimination of the differences expressed in the hierarchy of worth, privilege, role, status, and power that divided men and women. These were the differences with which the text is concerned.

During the time of the early church it was the common lot of women to play a second-class role in the society. Patriarchal control dictated that positions of leadership and importance were the domain of men. But the early church broke with this pattern in some significant, if not totally encompassing, ways. Elisabeth Schüssler Fiorenza has done important work in unearthing the previously hidden leadership roles of women in the early church.[1] It is clear from her work and the work of others that, although women were not totally freed from patriarchal control, they played a far more significant leadership role in the early church than was common for the broader culture of the time or than we have been led to believe by later interpretations and misinterpretations of scripture and history.

The hierarchical distinctions between men and women were challenged by the ideological paradigm and the social organization of the early church. Thus, Paul could write that in Christ there is neither male nor female, but all are one. And, as an increasing number of scholars are finding, this was more than simply wishful thinking. Women actually occupied a formidable place in the development of the early church.

That was because the church understood itself to be operating with a different view of the world and a different mandate from that of the dominant culture. The Book of Galatians tells us that the predominant laws and customs of the day were no longer the sole or even principal definers of the Christian's identity, nor did they set the terms for how Christians should organize their relationships. Christians have been set free to live out new lives under the conditions of a newfound freedom in Christ. The laws and customs of that culture defined people according to their roles, their nationality, their gender, and their place in the hierarchy. But the church discovered a new identity, and these old ways of understanding and organizing themselves were called into question.

Of course people did not suddenly eliminate their long-standing perceptions of national heritage, social status, or gender. The new paradigm did not result in instantaneous change; much of the old data continued to exist. The differences were still present in the early church. There were still slaves within the church as the letter to Philemon makes clear. There were still Jews and Greeks and Romans. There were still women and men. But the Epistle to the Galatians tells us that these factors were no longer the primary ones in defining their identity. And while things weren't perfect as a result of that new understanding, if we are to believe an increasing array of New Testament scholars, the break from the dominant definitions and customs was a reality. They were not limited to the old understanding or behaviors.

As Thomas Kuhn has pointed out in his work on scientific paradigms, there is a time lag between the development of a new paradigm and its influence on the broader scientific community. Most people continue to follow the old rules. They continue in their traditional behavior long after it is appropriate to do so.[2] He points to the common phenomenon of the use of science textbooks that are often years behind the newest scientific thinking and reflect nothing of the newer paradigms. Some scientists will even fight to maintain the old paradigm as many did in response to new thinking such as that of Copernicus or Galileo.

The early church was like that. Even though it was offered a new paradigm, namely, a system of belief based upon a freedom in Christ in which all the hierarchical distinctions were broken down, at its best it could embody this new understanding only partially. Tragically, according to Fiorenza, those who stood to benefit from the divisions were eventually able to gain control. They rewrote the history and interpreted it in such a way as to make invisible most of the new behaviors that had occurred.[3] What we have, as a result, is a rather innocuous-looking claim about our oneness with little explicit evidence of the remarkable behavioral changes that actually occurred.

A paradigm is a conceptual framework, but it always has behavioral consequences; it is always accompanied by organizational constructs. You cannot think in new ways without your behavior being affected, however gradual or painful the changes might be. A paradigm shift results in the reorganization of our world because every paradigm has organizational implications.

For example, there are a variety of paradigms that attempt to account for the fact that there are people of different skin colors. A racist paradigm posits a hierarchy of being. According to the paradigm of Western racism, Euro-Americans are considered to be more human, of higher worth, superior to people of color. When one adopts such a paradigm, then it follows that the society will be organized along the lines of hierarchical power relationships, that is, Euro-Americans over people of color.

The specific form of organization to express a given paradigm is contextually constructed. Apartheid is the specific South African form of political-economic organization that gives expression to a racist paradigm. Plantation slavery was our nation's initial political-economic form to express our racist paradigm.

In recognizing the important role of new paradigms in contributing to new behaviors and forms of social organization, I do not mean to imply the dangerous notion that ideas are *the* driving force of history. It is important to note that while paradigms influence behavior and social organization, the obverse is also the case. It is often the case that paradigms arise as ideological justifications or explanations for the existing power arrangements. In some ways we are back to the chicken and the egg debate. There is a dialectical relationship between ideas and behaviors, between paradigms and social organization; they feed each other, and often it is impossible to discern which is the source.

Sexism is a paradigm for explaining and handling the differences between women and men. It does so in a way that sets men higher than women on a hierarchy of being and importance. Patriarchy is a specific form of social organization related to a sexist paradigm. Sexism was the dominant paradigm and patriarchy was the pervasive form of social organization at the time of the early church. But just as there are other ways than the Ptolemaic system to understand the rising and setting of the sun, so within the church there developed other ways of understanding the world of women and men. The scriptures set forth an alternative paradigm, one born out of the egalitarian movement initiated by Jesus.

Perhaps the central New Testament paradigm for understanding our differences is captured by the metaphor of an organism. The differences are real, but they are like the different parts of the body, organically one, all of essential importance, but each with its own function. In the New Testament the body is a common metaphor for the Christian community. Ephesians, chapter 4, describes the process of maturation as one of a body, with Christ as its head, with all parts growing together. First Corinthians, chapter 12, describes the community as a body with various members, all vitally important and interdependent, with none more important than the other.

We have heard this before, of course. The slogan "unity in diversity" has been preached from our pulpits. The affirmation of pluralism within our society has been on everyone's lips. But we still face a serious problem, because the differences continue to be a source of division. We have not adopted a genuinely new paradigm for understanding our differences. We may have given lip service to a new way of thinking, but the fact that our society and churches remain organized along lines that continue to treat women, people of color, and the poor as inferior gives undeniable confirmation of our intransigence. Our society continues to treat differences as a basis for division.

We can also see this at work at the interpersonal level. Many marriages have begun because of each partner's initial fascination with the unique qualities and characteristics of the other. But often what fascinates eventually frustrates. Unable to affirm the differences of the other as enriching the relationship, one or both of the partners begins to demand that the other think and act just as they do. When this happens, the unity of the relationship drifts relentlessly into division.

The biblical paradigm recognizes and celebrates our differences. Differences are neither causes for division nor are they to be amalgamated in some melting pot. Differences and divisions are not the same thing. Divisions cut us off from one another. Differences are a gift to each other. Differences are the source of enrichment. Unity does not mean the end of differences.

Nor does unity mean the elimination of specialness or particularity. We can see this in the calling of Israel. Israel was called by God to be a special people, set apart, unlike the other nations. This constituted its particularity. However, that particularity was always for the sake of something universal—the blessing of the world. At their best, the children of Israel understood that they had been chosen, not for privilege but for service; to be a light to the nations, a blessing to all the people of the earth. This constituted their universality. They were different, special, set apart, but they existed for the sake of all and in relation to all.

There was always a tension between the particular (their specialness), which was reinforced by distinctive worship, codes, and geography, and the universal (their calling to be for the sake of the world), which was called forth in the prophetic movements. That tension between the particular and the universal is a central thread of Israel's history.

Tragically, in emphasizing its particularity, Israel often fell into the trap of division, interpreting its specialness as a mark of greater worth. Israel, at times, found itself so enthralled by its differences from the other peoples of the world that it interpreted its specialness as a prize, as a matter for boasting, as an occasion of privilege. And when it did so, when it wallowed in its own particularity for the sake of privilege, the prophets rose up to set forth the challenge of Yahweh.

> I hate, I despise your feasts, and I take no delight in your
> solemn assemblies. Even though you offer me your burnt of-
> ferings and cereal offerings, I will not accept them, and the
> peace offerings of your fatted beasts I will not look upon. Take
> away from me the noise of your songs; to the melody of your
> harps I will not listen. But let justice roll down like waters, and
> righteousness like an everflowing stream. (Amos 5:21–24)

The very rituals and music that constituted Israel's specialness
were rejected by Yahweh when these expressions were di-
vorced from the universal call to be for the sake of the world.

When specialness becomes a source of privilege rather than
a call to faithful service, it leads to division. It is good to
remember that holiness means being set apart for a special
purpose. In Protestant North America we have generally interpreted the word "holiness" to mean a certain kind of pious
purity, a renunciation of certain behaviors. Many have defined morality as personal purity and obscured the social dimension of justice. When we interpret holiness in that manner
it tends to lead to smugness and a sense of moral superiority.
And with a sense of superiority comes division. But when we
understand holiness to be a setting apart in order to be a
blessing to the world, then the call to faithful service leaves
no room for feelings of superiority and for division but leads
rather to humility and fundamental connectedness.

## Strategic Separations

Differences and distinctiveness need not lead to division. But
there is a certain kind of distinctiveness that raises some trou-
bling questions. What about those groups who emphasize
their particularity, focusing upon their differences with the
conscious intention of separating themselves from others?
Does unity leave room for Black Power, for Latino pride, for
militant feminism, and for the separation that each of these
movements has espoused?

Certainly any who have been on the outside of these movements knows how cut off, how divided, it feels. If our divisions are an expression of radical evil, a rejection of God's loving intent for our world, then what about these divisions? We have seen this happen time and again as African Americans, Hispanics, Native Americans, women, gays, people with handicaps, and others reject the dominant society. Are these separations simply further instances of sinful division, or do they have a legitimate place in the scheme of unity?

There are times when divisions (in a divided society) may function for the sake of eventual unity. It is important, however, to underscore that this can be the case only in a situation in which the sinful divisions already exist. In such a case, there are several circumstances when separation may lead to wholeness.

First, for our differences to be experienced as a gift by others, it is essential that they be allowed to blossom. Our distinctive histories, temperaments, cultures, biology, struggles and hopes, joys and sorrows, all need to be fully experienced and expressed. To offer ourselves wholly to another we must be in touch with what it is that makes us distinctively us. We cannot be content with simply playing a role, offering what we've been told we have to offer.

A marriage thrives when each partner gives to the other out of a sense of wholeness and specialness. Far too many people offer only what they think they are supposed to offer or what the other will accept, and in doing so both are shortchanged. No full relationship can be built out of partial offerings. To give ourselves wholly to another requires that we be fully in touch with who we are before we give ourselves to the other. Too many of us live out the roles that have been suggested for us rather than allowing our own gifts and specialness to transform those roles. No one wins in this situation. For the man to be limited to the role of provider and ruler is to stunt the development of his full gifts. For the woman to be limited to the role of nurturer and housekeeper is to stunt the development of her full gifts. And in doing so, the marriage relationship itself is stunted.

We can understand this when we think about two persons

in a relationship. But the same is often true for groups within a society. The divisions of our world have forced groups into societal roles that have constricted the development of their full distinctiveness. Groups, as well as individuals, are cast into roles.

For example, the divisions brought about by racism have systematically forced many persons of color to live out roles associated with the ascription of inferiority. It is common knowledge that our educational system is failing people of color in our cities. High dropout rates, students passed from grade to grade without mastering learning skills, run-down facilities, overcrowded classrooms, lack of safety in the schools, all contribute to deepening the hopelessness of young people in urban communities. A majority of our young people of color are denied the opportunity for the experience and expression of their fullness as persons, and many end up playing out the roles expected of them by our society: as dropouts, junkies, criminals, and unemployed. There are heroic exceptions, persons who grow to their fullness despite all odds. But the odds are against them.

In the face of these odds, some seek their specialness by going deeper into their oppression, by playing out with a vengeance the roles created for them by the society. While it is distinctive to be part of a gang, or a drug culture, it is a specialness born of and limited to the condition of deprivation.

The need to be special is undeniable. And often it is impossible to affirm one's distinctiveness without separating from those persons and structures that have forced one to live a lie. To experience and express one's own distinctiveness so as to discover the fullness of the gifts one has to offer, individuals or groups must sometimes separate themselves from the relationship that blocks them from blossoming. We recognize this need in a destructive marriage or in an unhealthy parent-child relationship. Many partners in marriage are unable to be whole because the relationship is oppressive. While a divorce can be extremely painful, it may also be liberating. So too, children who are thwarted in their development by a domineering parent may find that only in rebellion can they discover who they truly are.

It is the same in the larger society. When societal structures and paradigms do not permit the emergence of a person's or a group's differences and distinctiveness, then a divorce, a rebellion, or a separation may be essential. Just as divorce is a response to failure, so too is separation from society by various groups and individuals. If there were no crippling of persons and groups as the result of the fundamental divisions within our society, then these temporary and reflexive separations would not be needed.

In the face of such crippling, it is essential for persons and groups to reject imposed identities and structures and to uncover their stolen specialness, their buried history, their denigrated culture. Such a rejection and recovery necessarily constitutes a division. It is a division against those who have imposed the fundamental divisions. And it inevitably separates each person or group even from other oppressed persons and groups—for it is a journey that cannot be fully joined in by another.

A corollary of the necessity to separate in order to experience and express one's distinctiveness is the strategic need for regeneration. The kinds of divisions we experience within our society keep people on the defensive. We all end up fighting each other, expending our energies in competing for the crumbs. There comes a time for strategic retreat when most or all connections must be severed in order to take stock, to assess and gather strength. We know this necessity at the personal level. Jesus went off by himself for forty days into the wilderness. Many experience the importance of withdrawal from the fray through meditation and prayer, through retreats and extended periods alone. With the rare exception of contemplative religious and monks, though, we know that such a period is temporary, that we cannot remain forever in our private wildernesses. We eventually will have to return to the everyday realities and relationships we have temporarily set aside. But when we draw aside, it is an all-encompassing experience. We do not keep saying "this is only momentary," although deep down we know that. Most of the time we throw ourselves into separation with abandon.

Just as individuals need to separate at times, so, too, do groups. However, our society is quite selective in its appreciation of this need. There are some groups to whom we grant permission; usually they are the religious ones. However, when a group separates for political stocktaking and empowerment, many people get uptight. It is interesting to note which separatistic actions create alarm within the society. Most of the religious separatism is tolerated since it is assumed to pose no direct challenge to the paradigms and structures of the society. Monks and women religious can go off to their monasteries or convents without an eyebrow being raised. But if James Baldwin goes to France or some African Americans advocate a separate state, or women develop a course of study just for women, the tensions rise. Political separatists have usually been responded to with vehemence by the dominant powers. They are required to qualify every move and to reassure those who have been left out that it is only temporary, that things will return to normal.

This is because the dominant powers fear that the separation will result in the freedom of those whom they have dominated through division. Any person or group of people who discovers their own beauty and strength will not long allow themselves to be kept on the margins. Either things will change, or they will leave. Those who benefit from the existing divisions fear other kinds of division. They fear the strategic divisions of temporary separation that empower the marginal. And they fear the possibility of a division in which the marginal no longer are available to be oppressed.

Strategic separation to build up the strength to fight effectively and separation in order to discover one's worth are essential for survival and growth in a divided society such as ours. As with any division, however appropriately motivated, there is a danger of making one's separateness precious. One of the ways that this occurs is to assume an orthodoxy about one's separation. It is easy to fall into the trap of thinking that what is appropriate for one person or group is appropriate for all. Making our own decisions and actions the plumb line for all others leads to an arrogance that creates a fundamental division between us and others. This is the separatism that characterizes fundamentalism. Sadly, this is an all-too-familiar occurrence in the history of Israel, the history of the church, and the history of progressive movements for change.

## *Kairos and Separation*

The decision to engage in strategic division—separation for the sake of experiencing and expressing one's distinctiveness and for empowerment to struggle—is one that must be made on a case-by-case basis. There is no easy formula to apply to all circumstances. Such a decision must be made in terms of the *kairos.* There is a *kairos,* an opportune time for separation. Reading the signs of the times correctly is critical when affirming the time for separation.

The Greeks had two words for time; *chronos* and *kairos. Chronos* time is clock time. It provides a basis for predictability. "I will meet you for lunch at 12:15 P.M." Everyone knows what this means. *Kairos* time is unpredictable. It is the time of opportunity. You give birth according to *kairos,* not *chronos,* unless you've scheduled a cesarean section. The baby will emerge when it is ready. While there are signs to guide us, no one knows the moment of the event until it occurs. That's why so many parents find themselves in the oddest places when the *kairos* arrives. This is what Jesus had in mind when he refused to set a time *(chronos)* on the final days, which he said would occur only at the appropriate *kairos.* Such a time was unpredictable since it depended upon the convergence of many factors.

Since separation for the sake of ending the fundamental divisions of the society is decided by *kairos* time, it is impossible to set our watches, or to set watches for anyone else. Instead, it is absolutely essential that we develop the gift of discernment, the discernment of the signs of the times, in making such a decision. It is not a matter of following a formula, or wishing things to happen. There is no way that simply because it is someone else's time or some other group's time that it is our time. This is another way of saying that while we can learn from the experience of others we cannot automatically apply strategies derived from them. We may be helped to discern our situation because of their experience, but we cannot set our watches by them.

Since *kairos* is an opportunity or crisis, it is important to remember that it is not forever. Any separation should be for the eventual oneness that comes with the end of our divisions. The South African *Kairos Document* is itself a witness to this temporariness. After the white government banned the African National Congress in 1960, morale was at a low ebb. Many activists gave up hope. There was little pride or confidence about the possibilities of a different future. Black consciousness arose to fill the vacuum created by the banning of the African National Congress and through it the disenfranchised community found a source of pride in the face of apartheid's demeaning oppression.

But the separatism present within the Black Consciousness movement within South Africa did not last forever. Steve Biko understood that for apartheid to be conquered, all of its opponents—blacks, Indians, coloreds, and progressive whites—would have to work together. His death in 1977, allegedly the result of police beatings, catalyzed the momentum for a multiracial challenge to apartheid.

In our country the momentum for a genuinely united front against oppression is far weaker. Several things account for the difference. First, Euro-Americans constitute the majority in the United States. This removes a major source of power from the oppressed community, exactly the opposite of the situation in South Africa. Sheer numbers cannot be discounted as a serious factor in the equation of power. Second, our two-party system, which gives the appearance of a viable opposition, in fact makes almost any radical challenge seem unnecessary to the average citizen. The absence of fundamental differences between the Republican and the Democratic parties over issues of foreign policy, defense, and domestic economics remains unrecognized by most citizens. What minor differences do exist are interpreted as providing a real choice that obviates the legitimacy of, or need for, other parties. Third, much of our stated policy appears to be in favor of justice, quite contrary to the formal policy of apartheid. This means that the oppression within the United States is usually more *de facto* rather than *de jure,* making it more difficult to recognize.

Nonetheless there have been numerous attempts among the oppressed and the progressive groups within the United States to unite in a common challenge to poverty, racism, sexism, and other evils. But it is fair to say that all such attempts remain rather suspect and still marginal in the shaping of our society. Separatism of various sorts still carries the day.

In summary, differences can be a rich resource, and divisions are not always counter to unity and oneness. As we have seen, there is a difference between the divisions that are imposed in order to maintain unjust paradigms and structures, and the separations that are chosen. Separations that function for a limited time can often help us to recover the truth and provide a foundation for resistance to and transformation of destructive and dividing paradigms and relationships.

Unity in Christ does not mean the end of differences nor does it mean the rejection of all divisions. In fact, it may demand selective division through temporary separation in order to eliminate the fundamental divisions. In recent times, many of the movements directed by women and people of color have been shaped by a conviction that this is the *kairos* for separation. For more than twenty years now, separatism among various oppressed groups and progressive Euro-Americans has been the order of the day. Many of us have consistently supported this decision.

But now the question will not go away. Is this a different time? Are we in a new *kairos,* one in which the bonds of unity must be strenuously sought? In the light of God's intent for our oneness, in the light of the experience in South Africa, in the light of our own failure to reverse the tide of destruction, can we afford not to seek unity? Perilous as the task may prove

7. When have you been pressured to live out a role instead of being yourself? When was the last time you were surprised by someone who didn't act the way you expected?

8. Have you ever felt the need to separate yourself temporarily as an individual? As a member of a group? How does our culture view such separations? What is your opinion?

9. The appreciation of *kairos* requires the gift of discernment. How do we develop this gift?

# For Further Discussion

1. As you reflect on Galatians 3:28 as a biblical paradigm for liberation, what images of unity come to mind? What differences should remain? What differences has Christ abolished?

2. Considering Deborah, Huldah, Priscilla, and other biblical women in positions of authority, why have women been forced into relatively powerless roles in the church? Why do some "Bible-believing" churches refuse to ordain women?

3. Can you think of instances when Jesus challenged the accepted roles of women in his male-dominated culture? Has the church followed Jesus' example?

4. In accepting new paradigms, do you think the church is more or less open than society at large? Why? Is the church more likely to influence or to be influenced by the culture?

5. Racism is one paradigm for dealing with the reality of racial differences. What behaviors arise from a racist paradigm? What other paradigms deal with racial distinctions? Do different behaviors emerge from these?

6. What is meant by "unity in diversity"? How well has this been put into practice? What are the social/structural obstacles to unity in diversity?

7. Israel was set apart to be a special people in order to become a blessing to all people. Can you think of occasions when Israel rejected its uniqueness by trying to become like other nations? Can you recall stories in which Israel made the opposite mistake and strayed into racial/national chauvinism? How do Christians wrestle with similar tensions?

8. An African American teenager wore a T-shirt that said, "Before there was history, there was black history." What statement was the young man making? Have you ever felt the need to reclaim your special history or culture? Why or why not?

9. At a writing conference a room was set aside exclusively for women writers/conferees. How do you feel about this in the light of the discussion about temporary separation?

10. Differentiate between *chronos* and *kairos.* What happens when a *kairos* moment passes by unseized? Do you agree that this may be a *kairos* time for ending our separations? Why?

11. Is it oppressive or unfair if every job is given to the most qualified applicant? Explain.

# 3
# A Different Approach to Unity: Solidarity in the Struggle for Liberation

Although most attempts at unity have served only to maintain the divisions by keeping control in the hands of the dominant powers, many of us are still inexorably drawn to the vision. But we cannot be content with the old formulas and approaches. Given our history, the image of "one body in Christ" raises serious questions—questions that lead us into new territory.

I have suggested that a different way to think about unity is in terms of solidarity, specifically solidarity in the struggle for liberation.[1] As many Latin American Christians have come to recognize, "Christian unity thus begins to present questions very different [from] those we receive from Europe. . . . The paths which lead to accepting the gift of unity in Christ . . . are going through unecclesiastical places."[2] This recognition has emerged in the face of the indisputable class struggle that is going on in Latin America. There it is impossible to speak of Christian unity without at the same time being painfully aware of the enormous class divisions that exist within the society and of which the church is a part. Given this reality, solidarity has become the new mode of unity.

Since it is not commonly understood what is meant by the phrase "solidarity in the struggle for liberation," we will analyze the substance of each of its terms—solidarity, struggle, and liberation—in order to determine what promise there might be in such a new understanding.

Each of these terms is explicitly political and social, and appropriately so. But, as we shall see, each is also deeply personal, having to do with the most intimate aspects of our identity and relationships. And that too is appropriate, for if there is anything that has emerged clearly in recent theological discussion, it is that there is no possibility of separating the personal from the political, or the spiritual from the material. One of the most insidious consequences of the old idealistic philosophy is the division of the world into two realms: higher and lower, real and unreal, spirit and matter. The weight of scripture simply provides no room for such a bifurcation. Water and wine, sweat and spit, birth and death, marriage and friendship, armies and rulers, nations and families are all arenas in which the drama of salvation occurs. The Word becomes flesh. The Spirit works through the common stuff of life. The mind-set dominated by the speculative heritage of Greek idealism has led us to interpret scripture in a way that does injustice to its very intent.

This tendency to divide the world is so pervasive that it often catches us unaware. At a recent meeting of progressive church leaders to assess the current prospects for basic transformation in our society, one of the participants shared his feelings of hopefulness and hopelessness. He felt hopeful when he focused upon God, but hopeless when he focused upon humans. I think that I understood something of what was behind his feelings: discouragement in the face of the failures he has witnessed and a realization that the struggle for transformation requires a power that transcends the limits of our situation.

But it is impossible to separate God from humans when it comes to the possibilities of transformation. There will be no transformation without human faithfulness. Certainly transformation goes beyond our faithfulness, just as a genuine marriage of two persons involves more than their intent and efforts. There are always surprises, undeserved outcomes, unplanned growth. But, while human faithfulness cannot exhaust the possibilities for transformation, it is absolutely essential. We should not be naive. Evil is a reality; pride, greed, jealousy, sloth, and innumerable other frailties constantly raise their head. There is much to be disappointed about. But if we have lost all hope in human beings, we have lost all hope in the possibility of the transformation of our world. We cannot separate God and humans in the search for a transformed world.

And we cannot separate the personal from the social, the spiritual from the political in the search for unity. That is why solidarity, struggle, and liberation are multidimensional. Solidarity in the struggle for liberation is fully personal because it taps the roots of our identity and our relationships. Each of us longs to be reconnected, to not walk in fear, to reach out and enfold the other, even the stranger. Each of us longs to overcome our isolation. Even if we do not consciously think about our longings, they are evidenced by our nostalgia for a lost time of neighborhoods, of extended families, of small-town life. It is almost Christmas as I write this, and there is a mood in the air that exposes our desire for a world in which the divisions no longer exist. In much of the secularized Christmas story we are offered a picture of what was, or at least of what people would like to believe life was or could be. Scrooge becomes one of the Cratchit family. Families long separated sit before the fire, and crooks become honest citizens who care about the community.

While the lost days of which we are reminded may not have been as rosy as they are made to appear, the dimensions of bonding, care, and connectedness are extremely appealing. I would venture that in the United States the power of Christmas has more to do with this longing and promise of a reconciled community than it has to do with the original Christmas events. Our longing for unity is as deeply personal as any dimension of our lives, so the path to it must engage us at the most personal levels.

The path to unity necessarily involves us in political and structural issues as well. As we mentioned in chapter 1, the mechanisms that maintain our divisions are based on power and are deeply entrenched in societal structures. Simply longing for unity will not accomplish it. Good intentions in the face of structures of oppression will result in nothing more than disappointment and the perpetuation of oppression unless the intentions are accompanied by actions that directly address the structures that maintain the old order. Solidarity, struggle, and liberation inevitably involve us in politics.

We could approach these terms in any order, since each implies the other. We shall first consider "liberation," since that is the goal of our unity; second, "struggle," which is the means toward our unity, and finally "solidarity," which is the nature of our unity.

## Liberation as the Goal of Unity

To say that liberation is the goal of unity may raise some questions. Is not unity itself the goal? Didn't Jesus pray that his followers might be one as he and the Father are one? Isn't the atonement (the making "at one" of that which has been divided) the purpose of the life and death of Jesus? It would seem that unity is the very goal for which the creation groans. In a very important sense this is correct. To restore us to our rightful relationships—to reconcile us to God, to each other, and to our environment—is certainly what the gospel is about. In that sense it is appropriate to speak of unity as the goal itself.

When we consider, however, the efforts at unity that have taken place within the churches, we need to ask the critical question about the purpose or goal of such efforts. Too many attempts at unity have been for the sake of shoring up a faltering power base, or for maintaining the status quo. We need to be careful in affirming unity and reconciliation as our goal in the light of the church's history. We have seen how the pretense of unity has often camouflaged the actual goal of maintaining the status quo. When unity, understood as reconciliation, becomes the goal, it is easy to fall into wishful thinking and a false piousness that leaves us as divided as ever.

It is precisely the misuse of the concept of reconciliation that has helped to give rise to much of liberation theology. Nowhere is this seen more clearly than in James Cone's attack on J. Deotis Roberts' formulation of liberation as reconciliation.[3] Cone rejects all talk of reconciliation—at this point in U.S. history—as premature, as an evasion of the reality of racism and the necessary steps that must be taken to overcome it.

Given the way in which Euro-American Christians were so quick to adopt reconciliation as their slogan when the conflicts of the civil rights struggle emerged, one can understand Cone's rejection of liberation as reconciliation. Once the conflict surfaced, reconciliation became the cry. One evidence that reconciliation was simply a slogan rather than the encompassing goal of creation may be seen in the quick retreat from the struggle against racism made by the United Presbyterian Church beginning in 1969, only two years after it approved a momentous new confession of faith, the Confession of 1967. The cornerstone of that new confession was reconciliation. Yet within several years, its Commission on Church and Race was stripped of most of its powers.

Undoubtedly, many of the framers and supporters of the Confession of 1967 genuinely wanted unity and peace. The rebellions in our cities, the massive beatings and deaths of civil rights advocates, and the second-class citizenship afforded people of color in our society were all repugnant to them. However, what the Confession of 1967 championed was a reconciliation without fundamental structural transformation. It did not take seriously the painful necessity of the cross before new life becomes possible. Commendable as the vision was that it proclaimed, in failing to address the fundamental restructuring demanded by repentance it held out smooth words of promise—words that gained a ready hearing among the frightened Euro-American community. Everyone wanted to see the enmity and strife ended. Everyone was longing for unity. What the confession did not call for was a change of the basic order of things as a foundation for a reconciled people. As such, it followed in the line of all liberal do-goodism that wants things to be better without conflict and fundamental change. The reconciliation it offered was a pious wish. A deeply held wish, but a wish, nonetheless.

Given this history and the tendency to make unity a wish rather than a political project, we need a concept that will clearly emphasize the political/structural nature of our goal. Liberation does this.

One of the most central characteristics of liberation is its wholeness. It encompasses every dimension of our lives. Gustavo Gutierrez, the earliest Latin American systematic thinker to explore a theology of liberation, began his major treatise with a rejection of what he called the "distinction of planes."[4] Traditional theology divides life into different realms, some of which are more important than others. This follows the idealist's tradition. Gutierrez claimed that when we understand salvation in terms of liberation, then all of life, every facet of our existence, every dimension of the cosmos, is of ultimate importance and part of the drama of salvation.

Since liberation theology developed as a corrective to the dominant theologies that see the world as divided into spirit and matter, or heaven and earth, it is to be expected that it would emphasize not only the error of such division, but also the forgotten or formerly rejected aspects: the material, the political, and the structural. In so doing, liberation theology gained a reputation for not caring about "spirituality" and for being simply Marxist politics in religious disguise.

But such a claim is neither accurate nor fair. It is not fair in that all correctives have a tendency to overemphasize the dimensions that they are trying to recover. It is not accurate in that the developing literature of liberation theology has increasingly sought to explore the entire realm of experience, including what is today being called "spirituality." This is not only true among feminist theologians of liberation who have led the way in emphasizing wholeness, but also among many of the Latin American and African American liberation theologians as well as some interpreters of these theological communities.[5]

I have put the term "spirituality" in quotes because it is a problematic term for me. In too many cases what passes for spirituality is simply another form of the idealist's division of life into spirit and matter. It is my firm conviction that planning is just as spiritual as prayer, money just as spiritual as the still small voice, the disposition of armaments just as spiritual as the dispensing of the sacraments, and sexual expression just as spiritual as physical renunciation. Spirituality is not a quality that adheres to anything in itself. To be spiritual means simply to be "in the spirit." There is no aspect of life that is automatically in the spirit and none that is automatically excluded. To be spiritual means that our actions are intentionally working toward the goals of the spirit, that in the spirit we are groaning for the salvation of the world. To reduce spirituality to those actions that are designated as religious, private, and interior is to fall into the old dualism.

Liberation encompasses every dimension of our lives. The exodus tells of a liberation that involves the people in a new identity, the recovery of worship, a new name, a new land, new organizations, new economic arrangements, and a new mission. The Apocalypse of John promises that in the new heaven and new earth every tear will be wiped dry and a new city created. Both persons and structures will be attended to. Jeremiah is promised that the exiles will return to a restored Judah and Israel that are now in desolation. And the scope of Jeremiah's vision is all-encompassing: the restoration of family life, worship, laughter, singing, and economic control by the shepherds over their own flocks. Jesus weeps both for his friend Lazarus and for the city of Jerusalem.

Finally, this liberation involves the entire creation. The creation groans for its redemption. The liberation to which the scriptures bear witness is holistic. It links every aspect of life: the personal, the structural, and the environmental; the internal and the external; the family, the state, and the land; worship, economics, and ecology. There is nothing beyond its scope.

With such a vision of liberation as our goal, it is clear that the task before us demands unity. The goal encompasses the very unity we seek.

## Struggle as the Means of Unity

Something is working against the unity we seek. While analyses of the factors that stand in the way of our unity suggest varying explanations for our failure, it is commonly agreed that our divisions are the result of forces that seek to prevent our wholeness. Paul speaks of the principalities and powers; Marx speaks of class domination; contemporary therapists speak of co-dependency needs. In each of these and other explanations there are social structures in place that contribute to the inertia of our dilemma. I am increasingly convinced that any single explanation cannot do justice to the complexity of the forces aligned against us and that the problem is far more complicated than simply a failure of will or nerve on the part of individuals. We are caught in a web that can best be described as the politics of division, which inevitably involves us in conflict. As Paul Tillich maintained, it is redundant to speak of "power politics."[6] Politics implies the use of power, and power implies the use of politics. They are inseparable. And when power and politics are involved, inevitably there is conflict.

Politics, in this discussion, should not be understood as being limited to issues of voting, lobbying, and the choice of parties—what we commonly think of when we use the term. For our purposes, politics is much broader, more like the original Greek use of the term in which culture, family, economics, and government were all part of the *polis.* It is the social fabric, the network of structures that shape our lives, that we mean when we refer to "politics."

Since the unity we seek is in the context of our existing societal structures, it should come as no surprise that it will be born only in travail. There is an inevitable struggle that goes on when change is proposed. We know this to be true at a number of levels.

Many of us have been exposed to unfamiliar foods under circumstances that called for our gracious acceptance. The resistance to swallow what you had always thought to be inedible was one that you wondered if you could overcome. The battle raged: "Shall I risk offending my host—dare I put this in my stomach?" To bring ourselves to do things a new way, to try the untried, to break with tradition, often entails struggle. There is an inertia, a force that keeps us moving in the direction in which we have been going. It requires enormous energy to move in another direction.

Since making even such small changes is sometimes difficult, we should not be surprised at our resistance when demands are made to change the more fundamental aspects of our lives. That is why conversion is so difficult. Saul of Tarsus resisted and did not see the truth until he was struck blind. The alcoholic or the drug abuser knows the incredible struggle involved in deliverance from enslavement to the substance. Conversion involves a struggle against the inertia of our lives.

According to Thomas Kuhn,[7] it is the same in science. As we saw in the previous chapter, people resist new explanations and even resist seeking them. It is the rare scientist who, in the face of anomalies, will risk searching for a new paradigm. Most prefer to remain with the old theories and resist the new paradigms when offered, even when they know that there are serious problems with and limits to the accepted paradigm. He cites numerous scientists, such as Galileo, Newton, and Einstein, whose new paradigms were resisted by the majority of scientists when first offered.

It is the same in society. There is resistance to new ways of organizing our lives, new ways of relating, new ways of identifying ourselves. The Afrikaners, the minority of European ancestry who control South Africa, have resolutely resisted all efforts to bring about a change in the apartheid system that gives them control over the majority. Only through years of struggle have even the smallest changes been brought about.

The history of the modern People's Republic of China has been a seesaw of reforms and retrenchments, openings and closings. The massacre at Tiananmen Square in June 1989 was only the latest bout in the ongoing fight. Gorbachev's attempts to reform the Soviet Union through *glasnost* and *perestroika* met with resistance within his own country and in many other countries of the Eastern bloc. In all these cases, the old guard, the dominant powers, have not wanted to give up their hold, and the result has been enormous struggle.

The same is true of our own nation's history. The abolitionist movement was accompanied by civil war. The formation of labor unions was met with police and military repression. Women's suffrage engendered ridicule and repression. And civil rights for African Americans were achieved in the face of guns, dogs, fire hoses, and nooses.

Scripture confirms the centrality of struggle in the creation of a transformed world. Giving birth—a process of creation involving struggle and travail—is a central image for change in the Bible. Exodus from Egypt is accomplished through a conflict with pharaoh. The Promised Land becomes Israel's only through a series of battles with the Canaanites and surrounding nations. The apocalyptic imagery of The Day of the Lord that will usher in a new age is accompanied by upheaval. The Book of Revelation pictures the new heaven and new earth arising out of a cataclysmic war in Armageddon. Battle imagery is the dominant theme the apostle Paul uses to describe the nature of the internal and external struggle in which the Christian community is engaged. To fight that battle, he exhorts us to put on the whole armor of God. And Jesus once told his disciples that he had come not to bring peace, but a sword. From beginning to end, scripture points to the centrality of struggle in the coming of the new.

In the light of scripture, world history, and our own personal experience it is undeniably clear that the unity we seek cannot come about without struggle. But recognizing this is not enough, for there is a tendency within the church to deal with struggle as either a purely internalized personal experience or as something that occurs in another realm. The personalism and idealism of our Western tradition do not easily give up their control of the parameters of our thought.

There is no doubt that a struggle goes on within each of us when we are faced with understanding our world differently. This is more than simply the inertia of tradition. It goes to the very roots of our identity and meaning. Our identity is tied up with certain perceptions of ourself, our church, and our nation; when those perceptions are challenged, the foundation of our world is shaken.

In the late 1960s, the Brazilian educator Paulo Freire was doing consciousness raising at an East Harlem church with a group of Caribbean and Central American Hispanics, most of whom had come in search of prosperity. His method involved the use of slides depicting aspects of the lives of those with whom he was working. Over dinner one evening at my home, he told the story of how not one in the group correctly identified New York City as the location of a slide showing a garbage-strewn street corner. Instead, they named the cities from which they had emigrated. When asked if it could be a scene from New York, they rejected the notion "because this is America and this is a rich country."

They were shocked when he told them that the photo was taken just several blocks from the church. They had left home, family, and country to come to the United States for the promise of streets of gold. It was simply too much for them to admit that the belief that had carried them here was marred. To do so was to admit not only that the United States was wrong but that they were wrong.

Each of us knows the internal struggle that goes on when we are forced to deal with such recognition. The first time we discovered that our mother or father didn't know everything shattered our worldview. Putting things together without either a return to uncritical belief in them or a total rejection of them was a struggle. My belief in the United States as a totally generous world benefactor was shaken by my travels in Latin America in the early sixties. It was easier to deny my experiences and observations than to challenge my nationalistic perception. To face the challenge was a costly struggle. When we recognize the realities of our divided world, our identity is challenged, and we are cast into an unremitting struggle.

The struggle is not simply an internal one. It is impossible to speak of struggle without returning to the notion of "politics," the public arena. When we realize the nature of our divisions and their causes, we cannot ignore the fact that structures of power—economics, media, governments, education, the military, and religion—are integrally implicated. Overcoming our divisions is not simply a matter of thinking differently about others or ourselves. To be sure, that is inescapably involved. But, as we have seen, our divisions involve structures as well as attitudes. Both must be addressed, and to do so introduces struggle at the structural as well as the personal level.

Marx understood this and described the divisions in terms of class warfare. It has erroneously been assumed that Marx introduced the notion of class warfare and advocated it. This is incorrect. Rather, he unveiled the existing class warfare for all to see and advocated its destruction through the victory of the workers over the owners. While the complexities of modern capitalism and communism have altered the nature of our understanding of how classes work—many contemporary Marxists are wrestling with revising Marx in order to take into account these new realities—it is still true that class divisions permeate our world. Even among non-Marxists there is increasing alarm expressed in the media about the rapidly increasing gap between rich and poor in our nation. It is not uncommon today to read in the establishment press warnings of class divisions similar to those raised by Marx over one hundred years ago.

It has frequently been stated that struggle does not necessarily imply violence. There are various ways in which the struggle for transformation occurs. But given our penchant for leaping immediately to the issue of violence, it is important to note that violence is already present. It is the preexisting condition out of which the struggle is born. Our oneness has been violated by violent means. Millions within our nation are violated every day through impoverishment, lack of resources, discrimination, and physical abuse. Our divisions are a violation of God's intent, a violation of our nature as human beings. And these divisions are perpetrated and maintained by violent means. This is the context in which struggle for a transformed world takes place. It is important not to reverse the order of things. The struggle is against existing violence.

The unity we seek will inevitably involve us in struggle: the internal struggle that accompanies new questions, new understandings, new allegiances, and the public struggle that comes with challenging the structures and persons that maintain the divisions and separate us from our true destiny.

## Solidarity as the Nature of Unity

In 1975 a gathering of progressive Christians from North America and Latin America was held in Detroit. It was the beginning of Theology in the Americas and was spearheaded by an exiled Chilean priest, Sergio Torres, a man of incredible charisma, energy, and vision. The dream that drew us together was of a church and a progressive social movement that would cut across all racial, gender, and nationalistic lines. We understood that the differences among us could no longer be allowed to prevent us from common action. And so we came together, all four hundred of us. We came from every corner of the United States and Canada, from Central and South America, and the Caribbean, from every denomination, and all walks of life. It was a heady moment, with many of the great names in liberation theology from Latin America and our own country gathered in one spot. It was the beginning of a network for dialogue, analysis, and publication. While there were problems and conflicts, the mood was extremely positive. The presentations were inspiring, the working sessions productive, the worship enriching, and the informal fellowship encouraging.

After lunch one day a few of us left the convent in which the conference was being held. We walked through the downtown Detroit neighborhood, a section that was marked by the ravages of poverty. We were a mix of the church itself: women and men, several Latinos, one Native American, one African American, and three or four Euro-Americans. As we walked, one of our group was struck on the back by an object and let out a surprised cry. Soon, rocks were hurling down all around us, several hitting their mark. We looked back and up. A gang of youths was behind us and on the rooftops above. We began to run—filled with conflicting feelings. We were scared and angry, yet at the same time we felt connected to them and their plight. Although we wanted them to know that we were in solidarity with them, that we weren't the enemy, what we did was run.

Our intentions were not enough. Something critical was missing. The anger and violence of those young people forced us to ask ourselves the meaning of solidarity. We were serious, or at least we were trying as best we could, but our presence precipitated rage rather than appreciation among the youths. What does it mean to be part of the church that wants to work for transformation, for justice, healing, and peace in a society that is torn apart by destructive divisions? What is solidarity in a divided society?

## Solidarity as Friendship

I have chosen the term "solidarity" quite consciously because it is linked with protest and revolutionary movements around the world; whether in Poland, or Nicaragua, or South Africa. It is a term that implies politics, and appropriately so, given the scope of liberation.

Solidarity also implies something beyond what we normally consider politics; it implies friendship. Friendship is a form of bonding between people that involves the depths of our being. It goes beyond the calculations that often characterize relationships that are primarily or exclusively task oriented. Friendships are intimate, vulnerable, faithful relationships. Beverly W. Harrison describes solidarity as "continuous relationship, fidelity to relationship, and mutual accountability

. . . it is a shared resistance to all that threatens life's promise."[8] Many of these characteristics have also been used to describe marriage: continuous, faithful, mutual relationship. There are other dimensions that I think need to be added: namely, respect and affection. Solidarity is a process, as is marriage, that involves loyalty, ongoing commitment, and mutual accountability. Genuine solidarity involves us at two levels, the structural and the personal. Neither in itself is enough. The structural level of solidarity is that of political alliance, and the personal level of solidarity is that of friendship. At that moment in Detroit we were attempting to be in political alliance, but we certainly were not friends. The stone throwers did not even know our names, let alone our intention to be in solidarity with them. They had not participated consciously in our dialogue. At best our confrontation was only a beginning: we knew they existed.

Perhaps by drawing upon the biblical notion of the covenant we can better understand the dual dimensions of solidarity as political alliance and personal friendship. When Yahweh entered into a covenant with Israel, it was an act of solidarity that involved politics and friendship. Yahweh would be there for them as their shield and buckler, to defend them against the arrows of their enemies. He would be their political ally. It also meant that he would be there to hear their cries, dry their tears, and receive their joy. He would be their friend.

Because the covenant was a relationship of friendship as well as political alliance, it was a relationship of mutuality; a mutuality far deeper and more vulnerable than simply the trade-offs that one power makes with another. This was not simply "I will do this if you will do that," the way contemporary political treaties are made or the way that some of the Deuteronomic writers would have us think of the covenant. Rather, the story of God's covenant with Israel and with the church is far more personal—and mutual—much more a relationship of friends.

Many Christians have lost sight of the mutuality implicit in God's solidarity with us because of an emphasis upon God's sovereignty. Certainly there is much within the scriptures that points to God's sovereignty, but the emphasis upon a God who sets and controls the agenda of history is at best only part of the biblical picture, and not the dominant part, at that. When we examine Yahweh's covenant with Israel, we find that it was a relationship of mutuality. Sometimes Yahweh was the initiator, as in the Creation or when Yahweh appeared to Moses in a burning bush. Even in the latter event, however, we are told that Yahweh's appearance was in response to the cries of the people. At other times the people were the initiators, as in Abraham's intervention on behalf of Lot or Moses' bargaining with Yahweh. The covenant was kaleidoscopic, involving alternating initiatives, anger, repentance, and arguments. Only when Yahweh and Israel stood side by side as friends could the purpose of the covenant—the blessing of the world—be accomplished. A covenant is a solidarity relationship that involves political alliance and the mutuality of friendship.

Solidarity as friendship is a loving relationship based upon choice. We become friends not out of convenience or because we are forced to but because we care about the other. We find that we are drawn to others out of respect, empathy, similar concerns, shared visions and, often, just plain chemistry. A friendship must be reciprocal, but it need not and often cannot be equal. Solidarity recognizes that the other may have less to offer at the moment; that was certainly true of Israel and Yahweh. And that is all right. What is not all right is for solidarity to be a one-way street; the blind allegiance of a follower to an all-powerful leader. Solidarity, as friendship, involves mutuality, however uneven and shifting that mutuality may be.

It is interesting to note that the relationship between God and those in solidarity with God often is spoken of in terms of friendship. Isaiah 41:8 refers to Abraham as the friend of God. Because they were friends, negotiation and arguments were possible, and God and Abraham changed in the process. Abraham left his home, changed his name, and took up a new vocation. God backed down from indiscriminate and immedi-

to be, is there not greater peril in continuing on our current path? If our answer, however tentative, leads us in the direction of unity, then it remains for us to explore the nature of such unity and how it might be achieved.

# For Reflection

1.  New ways of understanding the world are slow to be accepted. Why do people cling to outdated paradigms? How has your thinking changed in regard to science? history? cultural values?

2.  Our actions affect our thinking, and vice versa. A change of attitude led to the abolition of slavery in America; and abolition encouraged new attitudes toward African Americans. What actions or experiences have changed your attitudes? What new attitudes have influenced your behavior?

3.  The biblical model of the body encourages mutuality and respect for differences. How does this model differ from the sociological theory of structural functionalism? What role does power play in each paradigm?

4.  Have you ever been in a relationship enriched by interpersonal differences? A relationship that was damaged by differences? When you meet a person for the first time, what kind of differences do you find exciting? What differences are threatening or uncomfortable?

5.  Holiness means being set apart for a special purpose. In John 17:10–19 Jesus prays for God to sanctify his followers. Does the passage suggest the purpose for which Christians are to be set apart?

6.  Temporary separation may be a healthy means to nurture the blossoming of our distinctive gifts. Do you have gifts that you have been afraid to offer to others? Has this happened to you in your family? In your workplace? In your church? What would encourage you to offer these gifts to others?

solidarity. When solidarity is understood only in terms of strategic politics, anyone or anything can be treated simply as something to be exploited.

We can cite numerous instances in which individuals, racial groups, or even entire nations have been reduced to fodder for strategic political considerations: the Native Americans of the United States and of Latin America, the Africans brought over as slaves, the political scapegoats of the McCarthy era.

We have done the same with nature, losing sight of the consequences for the life systems that sustain us. That is what modern technology has become in the service of economics and nationalism—the use of the resources of nature without consideration of anything other than profit and power. Solidarity as friendship opens the door to an awareness of our universe as more than simply a means to an end. The universe is not simply a resource, it too is our friend. When we understand this, to be in solidarity with nature is not simply to dominate it as Western culture has tended to do; it is to be in a relationship of mutuality and reciprocity, in the I-Thou relationship of which Martin Buber has so eloquently spoken.[10]

The doctrine of an all-powerful, sovereign God has contributed significantly to our Western culture's loss of a sense of relatedness to nature and to each other. For those looking for models of domination, it has served as a justification for a hierarchical approach to life: God dominating humans, humans dominating "inferior" humans and nature. For those looking to escape responsibility, it has served as a deliverance: we are simply responders.

We can understand the appeal that an omniscient, omnipresent, omnipotent God offers and understand the circumstances that give rise to such an emphasis. When the avenues of progress are blocked, when all human promises seem empty, when the future appears unremittingly destructive, we search for consolation and hope. Karl Barth's crisis theology was just such a response to the failed optimism associated with the beginning of the twentieth century. When World War I and the worldwide economic depression that followed shattered the dreams of those who thought they were building the kingdom of God on earth, Barth recovered the reformed and Augustinian emphasis upon the sovereignty of God. While an emphasis upon a sovereign God who controls history may give consolation to those in despair, it can also lead to a sense that we are simply responders to, not shapers of, our lives and history. It can work against the possibility of solidarity, for solidarity involves a greater mutuality than this doctrine implies.

Mutuality may be fine in theory, but what does it mean in the real world? What does it mean to speak of solidarity as friendship when we are talking about African Americans and Koreans, Latinos and Euro-Americans, gays and straights, women and men, the temporarily able and the disabled? This will be the focus of the next chapter when we consider paths to unity. But let me mention briefly three implications for seeking friendship across our divisions. First, it means that we have to recognize that there are different kinds and levels of friendship. Second, we have to deal with the political realities that prevent friendship from blossoming. Third, we have to accept the reality that sometimes politics will precede friendship.

We have various kinds of friends. The common distinction we make between acquaintances and close friends recognizes that we relate on different levels. Sometimes this is simply the result of the time we can spend with the other. Sometimes there is an automatic connection that occurs, a spark of attraction that is compelling, drawing us toward each other. Sometimes we are brought together by an immediate need, and when the need is past we find ourselves together only occasionally. Such factors as age, family circumstances, profession, life cycle stages, and geography also contribute to determining who our friends will be and the nature of those friendships. We cannot expect every friendship to be alike or any particular friendship always to remain the same. It is enough that each friendship offers the aspects it does.

Even with those whom we would call our dearest friends, we do not share totally. There are always recesses hidden to others and even to ourselves. Furthermore, we choose to share parts of ourselves with some, parts with others. This does not constitute a failure of friendship but rather indicates the variable patterns that friendships take. If we quantify the concept of friendship and reserve the designation for those with whom we share a certain amount or aspect of our lives, we shall find our prospects for friendship quite paltry.

Yahweh's friendship with the covenant people of Israel took different forms at different times and with different members of the community. Consider the way in which Yahweh related to the people of Israel as a friend: sometimes weeping for them, sometimes roaring at them, sometimes comforting them, and always holding back something of the fullness of Yahweh's being.

Jesus was a friend to his disciples and to other followers such as Mary and Martha. But Jesus took only a few of the disciples to the garden to watch and pray with him in his final hours. And only Mary knew the intimacy of anointing Jesus.

The kinds of friendships that develop in the context of solidarity also vary. Our languages, personal histories, sexual orientations, cultural mores, and temperaments all contribute to differences of expectation, perspective, sensitivities, and understanding. That we can come together and find mutuality across these and other differences is a gift of grace and points to the power of and our longing for friendship. There can be no formula for the friendship dimension of solidarity—certainly not the romantic notions of friendship that abound in our society. In many ways we are treading on new territory in seeking friendship across the lines that have so long divided us.

For many Euro-American males models of friendship are severely limited: relationships with men are frequently characterized by the locker-room syndrome, with women by the consumption syndrome. The locker-room syndrome forces men to constantly hide behind the mask of machismo: men must be powerful, nonvulnerable, in control, cavalier. The consumption syndrome forces men to deal with women as simply means to their ends. In either case there can be no friendship because there is no reciprocity.

Sometimes men extend these models to their attempts to be in solidarity. Hiding behind the pretense of being on top of things, having things under control, being cool or "with it" are common experiences for many men when relating to those who have been marginalized. In fact, it is difficult not to carry locker-room training into all of a man's relationships. The consumption temptation is equally present, using the relationship with the marginalized to serve selfish needs: to buy merit or forgiveness so that a man may feel good about himself.

Friendship, however, involves caring for and about the other. It means bothering to know what it is she or he is experiencing, as best we can understand. It means attentiveness to the other. Attentiveness is different from understanding. Often we cannot fully understand what the other is experiencing or feeling—especially when we have been prevented from knowing the other by the divisions that abound—but we can continue to be there with them, to attend to them with empathy. In the attending we may discover something of their experience, something of their longing, struggles, and gifts. And that becomes a basis for our sharing and the deepening of our solidarity.

## Solidarity as Political Alliance

Solidarity also entails politics. It is not enough to want unity. Most of us are uncomfortable with the divisions and would like everyone to like everyone else. Things would be so much more pleasant then. However, simply wishing to be friends may make us feel virtuous, but it will accomplish little or nothing. Until we are able to attack directly the racism, poverty, class exploitation, patriarchy, and other sources of our divisions, we shall remain harmless dreamers.

One of the great temptations within modern Christianity is to think that the spoken word is a disembodied truth standing on its own. Because we have thought it or said it, we assume that things are so. But that is not the meaning of a true word. A true word is connected to the one who utters it and in the uttering it is connected to the one addressed. A false word is one that does not arise from the depth of the speaker and has no inextricable connection with the one addressed. Locker-room talk is a false word. Neither the speaker nor the one addressed is changed by its utterance. The posturing, the masks, remain. Consumption talk is a false word. Neither is changed. The words "I love you" have often been uttered simply to seduce rather than to express one's depth of emotion. The true word comes from one's deepest longings and joys and touches the other's deepest longings and joys, and in the sharing, each is changed.

Much of contemporary Christian talk is a false word. Prayer that allows the speaker and the one addressed to remain unchanged is false. To think that because we have prayed the matter ends there is erroneous if there is something that we can do. Only when prayer involves us in doing all that we can is it true prayer. In the same way, statements of belief that cost us nothing are false. To believe that God longs for the reconciliation of the world means that we must do all that we can to bring about that reconciliation. Anything less is a false statement.

Much of our talk about unity is a false word because it costs us nothing, it involves no change in us and no action to change the basis of the divisions. It is not sufficient to speak of unity or solidarity. To long for solidarity as friendship inevitably thrusts us into the political struggle against that which prevents our oneness.

We need to engage in the political level of solidarity even when we have not yet achieved friendship. That is what was being attempted in Detroit. Even among the conference participants themselves political action was being explored while friendships were yet in the making.

The fact is that we cannot expect friendships among the divided to be built in the absence of or before political engagement. Sometimes that may happen, but the odds are against it. Too many promises and good intentions have fallen by the wayside when the going got tough, too many warm words of friendship have turned hollow in the face of reality. As Jesus said, "not every one who says to me 'Lord, Lord' shall enter the kingdom of heaven" (Matt. 7:21). Pledges of friendship become empty words in the absence of faithful action.

What this means in the quest for oneness is that we will have to work together even before we like or trust each other. The level of friendship will need to be built within the context of political alliance. Under these circumstances it is to be expected that agreements will be reached cautiously, actions will be watched and judged, information will be guarded, and leadership will be disputed.

If we wait until we trust and like one another we will wait forever, as the divisions will keep us in permanent distrust and suspicion. We must begin with strategic political action as the basis of friendship. On the other hand, if we do not move beyond strategy and action to the building of friendship, we will find that our alliances become the occasion for new divisions.

In 1974 I was hired by a coalition of seminaries to develop and direct an urban ministry concentration, based in New York City, for master of divinity students.[11] From the beginning it was clear that we wanted a genuinely pluralistic student body and faculty with a commitment to liberation. One of my first tasks was to find an African American pastor with similar concerns and good teaching skills who could help to shape and work with the program. A man was recommended, and we arranged to meet in Riverside Park. As we began to share what we might hope for such a program, our differences became evident. Our different visions arose out of our radically different life journeys and communities. By the end of our conversation we were clear that we did not trust one another and that this was not a match made in heaven. We left on hostile terms.

Mutual friends prevailed upon us to get together one more time to see if we couldn't come to some agreement about a program and goals, even if we didn't particularly like one another. We did, and that began a seven-year working relationship that brought about one of the most creative educational ventures in seminary training in the United States and one of the deepest friendships I have known. But the building of the friendship took time and grew out of our common task.

To realize that friendship may follow political action should not come as a surprise. When we think about it, many of our friendships develop out of shared activities. A stranger is invited to be a fourth for tennis, and we hit it off. We walk side by side at a demonstration and strike up a conversation that leads to sustained connection. We work at the same job and discover we have similar aspirations, gripes, and interests, and we begin to spend time together after work. Shared activity often precedes friendship.

Perhaps solidarity demands something more like an arranged marriage than one based upon romantic love. There has been no context for courtship; in fact, we haven't spent any time together, and we know nothing of the other. To walk up and expect friendship to develop as if we've each been overcome by some magical potion is the stuff of fairy tales. Even when the buds of friendship begin to appear between persons or groups who have been divided, all of the dynamics surrounding us tend to pull us apart. In an arranged marriage the union is strategic and the development of friendship and love follows, slowly built over time while living and raising a family together. In our romantically oriented society such arrangements are looked upon with disdain. So, too, in the broader society we tend to operate romantically, hoping or expecting that we will be able to overcome our divisions, become friends, before doing the hard work of politics. But experience would suggest that this is not the way.

All the while, though, it is friendship for which we long. We are incomplete without the other; our growth is stunted. Because we have tasted the richness of sharing across the divisions, we know that there is something better in store for us, and we are impatient to live this way all the time.

New York Theological Seminary has frequently become the context for friendships arising out of common actions. Most of our students have been engaged in ministry for many years. Most are going to school later in life and have lived with the harsh realities of the metropolitan area. Half are African

American, a quarter are Latino and Asian or Asian American, and a quarter are Euro-American. In sharing our lives and ministries we sometimes discover our solidarity in action, a solidarity that perhaps had remained hidden to others. When we discover each other's concerns and commitments, we occasionally let down our defenses and, in grace, reach out across the seemingly insurmountable barriers. The power of such an experience is overwhelming. Nothing else seems to matter at the moment. The divisions have disappeared, if only temporarily, and we are whole. This is a day of the Lord such as that spoken of in reference to Pentecost in Acts, chapter 5. Or perhaps it is only the "moment" of the Lord. Whatever it is, it is undeniably what we are meant to be. When we know these moments, we are forever discontent with the divisions.

We see this same reality in South Africa, where some of the divisions have fallen, not completely, to be sure, but significantly. Blacks, coloreds, Indians, and progressive whites have come to understand the critical importance of strategic unity for the sake of liberation. In the process, many who never knew one another before have become friends. This is what is so dangerous for the dominators who oppress the majority: not simply that strategies and actions are developing, but that friendships are being forged that will not be crushed. The words of Jesus take on increased meaning: "Greater love has no one than this, than that a person lay down one's life for a friend" (John 15:13, author's translation). When politics develop into true friendship, then the politics deepen to the point of the cross. It is at the cross where politics and friendship meet. The power of politics and friendship combined can change the world.

Solidarity in the struggle for liberation means that we who have been divided have been so captured by the aperitif and vision of our oneness that we no longer are content to live under the old definitions, identities, and arrangements. We have experienced moments of unity, and we now know the purpose for which we have been created. With this compelling vision, we engage in a struggle against the powers that divide us in order to liberate ourselves and others from the tyranny of our divisions. We do this as people of the *polis* and as friends.

Sometimes it seems that we shall never see the day when nation shall not rise up against nation, when brother or sister shall not rise up against brother or sister. Nevertheless we are compelled to claim the unity that is promised, and we cannot give up simply because the way is long and arduous. And so we press ahead to the prize of our high calling.

With this vision and resolve we need now to explore the ways to solidarity.

# For Reflection

1.  Many Christians seem to express their faith exclusively either in the political arena or in the personal realm. Why are the two areas of faith so seldom integrated? How does each inform and enlarge the other? Do you tend in one direction? How could you broaden the practice of your faith?

2.  "There will be no transformation without human faithfulness." What does this statement mean to you? Do you agree?

3.  Genuine repentance must precede reconciliation. The biblical concept of repentance involves a "change of mind" and a "change of direction." How do these ideas address the quest for reconciliation between oppressors and oppressed?

4.  "Liberation encompasses every dimension of our lives." Mark 2:1–12 tells the story of Jesus' healing of a paralytic. How is the man's inward life addressed by Jesus? His physical needs? His economic situation? How is Jesus' act a challenge to the oppressive structures of his day?

5.  In what areas of life are you most resistant to change? The personal? The social? At home? At work? At church? What factors help you to welcome change?

6. Would you agree that oppressed minorities are victims of institutional and social violence? How are ghettos an example of cultural violence? What about unemployment? Substandard educational opportunities? Derogatory media images? Can you add other violations to the list?

7. Does the church overemphasize the sovereignty of God? Is the sovereignty of God consistent with God's friendship with humankind? How can a friendship be reciprocal but not equal?

8. Friendship presupposes the sharing of strength and vulnerability. How do we experience the vulnerability of God? With your friends is it easier for you to be the helper or the helped?

9. Will attentiveness to another always lead to understanding? If not, what is the value of attentiveness?

10. Have your friendships been hampered by racism? Classism? Sexism? How many of your friends are markedly different from you?

11. Desmond Tutu has said that a person becomes a person only through other persons. How does friendship help us grow toward completeness? Is there a friend who has helped you grow?

# For Further Discussion

1. What is the danger of confusing liberation and unity? Why is unity an insufficient end in itself? What groups might reasonably be suspicious of cheap offers of reconciliation?

2. Christmas brings to the surface our longings for connectedness and restored relationships. What other occasions or seasons in life arouse similar feelings? Can such moments lead to true restoration?

3. What does it mean to say that every area of life can be spiritual? Are all jobs considered to be spiritual tasks in your church? Should they be?

4.  Oppression of the earth ultimately threatens the oppressors themselves. Is this true of other instances of oppression?

5.  The author tells the story of a group of Hispanics who were shocked into revising their vision of America. Has your view of this country changed over the years? In what ways? Did such change involve inner struggle?

6.  Solidarity involves both political alliance and friendship. What are the shortcomings of politics or friendship alone as means of uniting people?

7.  The divine covenant with Israel was an act of solidarity embracing politics and friendship. Could you express the Christian covenant in the same terms?

8.  Can God's mind be changed by human actions? Consider how Moses intercedes for Israel in Exodus 32:11–14. Would you characterize Moses and God as friends?

9.  We usually think of prayer as the sharing of our longings with God. What longings does God share with us? Can we learn of God's longings apart from prayer?

10. What different kinds of friendship have you experienced? Why do levels of friendship vary? How does this apply to solidarity between diverse groups?

11. "Statements of belief that cost us nothing are false." What kind of confessions are costly? What beliefs have been costly for you?

12. How was the cross an act of friendship? Of politics? Is God political?

# 4
## Paths to Solidarity

If unity is understood as solidarity in the struggle for liberation, then we are faced with a significantly different set of problems than those normally associated with ecumenical relations. We are forced to deal with issues of strategy and personal relationships that have seldom been part of the traditional ecumenical enterprise. We are sailing in uncharted waters, with little to guide us, hence, we will have to take some risks.

The goal of unity is our starting point, but it is only the beginning. There is no agreement among us as to what constitutes solidarity. I have suggested that it means at least friendship and political alliance, but a fuller understanding of the meaning of solidarity will come only as we work together. And there is no agreement as to how to get there. That too will develop only as we share and work together. Despite the open-endedness of our quest for unity, we are certain about its rightness. As divided as we are, we all long for the day when the walls of alienation will crumble. So, like Joshua and his companions, we keep marching, wondering if we're not a little crazy to think that our meager efforts can bring the walls tumbling down. Still, we march, knowing that the power of our longings cannot finally be denied because it is not simply our longing but the longing of the entire creation and the longing of the Spirit of God who groans with us in the midst of our divisions.

It is not just any unity we seek, but the unity that results when people have been set free from the bonds that enslave them, when they can freely choose their name, the God they will serve, where they will live, and with whom they will journey. We seek the unity that is the result of liberation.

The journey toward unity assumes a willingness to struggle. Anyone who engages consciously in the struggle for liberation and unity does so with some significant costs. It would be far easier to avoid all this—to spend our lives playing the game as we've been programmed. While it is fulfilling to struggle for liberation and to work for solidarity, it is never easy and often quite painful. To do so is to place oneself intentionally in situations of mistrust, disagreement, and tension. It is easier to remain with "one's own kind." It is easier to stay within the comfort zone, not to expose oneself to rejection or automatic suspicions, not to have to bear the sins of one's parents to the third and fourth generation, not to have to keep reopening old wounds, not to have to be self-conscious about one's own complicity and ignorance. To wrestle continuously with these divisions is exhausting and often infuriating.

However, if we believe that we are called to be one, there is no other way. The divisions will not go away magically. No one will love or trust us automatically just because we express empathy or claim to be on their side. Political alliances and friendship take time and involve significant cost. Only as we are compelled by the vision of our oneness, and only when we are convinced that things do not have to remain as they are, will we find the strength to persist in the struggle.

The story of Ruth reveals this basic truth. Knowing that there was no place for widows and foreigners in Judah, Naomi encouraged her Moabite daughters-in-law, Ruth and Orpah, to remain in Moab and return to their families after the deaths of their husbands rather than accompanying her to her own homeland of Judah. Orpah did as her mother-in-law suggested, but, as recorded in one of the most beautiful passages in scripture, Ruth refused to leave her.

> Entreat me not to leave you or to return from following you; for where you go I will go, and where you lodge I will lodge; your people shall be my people, and your God my God; where you die I will die, and there will I be buried. May the LORD do so to me and more also if even death parts me from you. (Ruth 1:16–17)

Ruth's strength to deal with the divisions that her widowhood and alien status entailed came from her compelling love for Naomi and from her trust that the future in Judah did not have to be as they feared, as long as they were together.

The road to solidarity is a long one and filled with pitfalls. We cannot insist upon purity, for that is beyond any of us. The divisions run too deep for us to escape them easily, if at all. As Paul did, we experience a war going on within us. (See Romans 7:15–20.) The good that we would do, we don't, and the evil we would not do, we do. The scars of racism, sexism, and nationalism may never totally disappear. They are deep within us. Sometimes we are overtaken, as if by a thief in the night, by long-rejected stereotypes and feelings. If we expect purity from ourselves, we will wallow in guilt and self-pity. If we expect purity from others, we will continuously stand in judgment, unable to accept and love them. The path to solidarity will be impossible to take if we do not learn to forgive ourselves and others for the contradictions and failures in our journeys.

Having said this, what is the way ahead? What are the paths to solidarity? To try to answer this question is at best presumptuous and at worst foolish. Nonetheless, I am compelled to share my experiences and ideas, not as *the* answer, but as part of an ongoing dialogue for the sake of a transformed world.

Each of us is accountable for faithful stewardship of what we have been given. In Matthew 25, Jesus uses a parable to describe the basis for God's judgment. Several stewards were left in charge of the master's wealth while he was away. Upon the master's return he asked for an accounting. The one who had been entrusted with five talents had doubled them through wise investment. But the steward who had been given one talent timidly hid it, fearing to risk it and the potential wrath of his master. Upon discovering this, the master punished him for not wisely using what he had been given.

Each of us lives with givens, things we cannot change. Our birth gives us our race and gender. Class background paves or blocks the way to opportunities in education, employment, and so on. We cannot change our skin. Nor do we have control over how and where we were raised and the opportunities this afforded or prevented. We are not responsible for these things, and it does no good to flagellate ourselves for what we cannot change. This is our fate. But we are responsible for what we do with what we have been given. The issue is not one of birth but of options.

Liberation theology emphasizes the fact that God comes to us in Jesus the Galilean, the nobody from Nazareth. In Jesus we have revealed the truth that God is on the side of the oppressed. But even Jesus' identification with the poor and marginalized involved options and not simply birth. Jesus could have been born in a far more oppressed condition. He could have been born a woman, or a cripple, or a leper. Instead, he was born a healthy son of a craftsman. Philippians 2:5–8 tells us that Jesus emptied himself—gave up the privileges that were rightfully his—and became a servant and was crucified. The self-emptying of Jesus, his identification with the outcasts of his society, was not because of his birth, but because of the choices he made: whom he lived with and cared for, whom he challenged, whose side he took. Even for Jesus, solidarity was dependent upon his choices, not the givens of his birth.

I speak out of the experience of growing up as a straight, Euro-American male of middle-class working parents in the suburbs of Philadelphia. My formation was influenced by the nationalism of World War II, the anticommunism of the

McCarthy era, Northern racism, the economic expansionist dreams of the Eisenhower postwar boom, and Protestant fundamentalism. My world was racist, misogynist, anticommunist, anti-Catholic, homophobic, anti-Jewish, and abounded in certainty that our country was the God-appointed savior and guardian of the world. These were some of my "givens."

Those of us whose race, gender, class, and nationality have shaped us in such ways do not have to remain myopic, however. We are offered the option of new ways of understanding and being that come with different experiences of the world. My own myopia was shattered by my experiences in Latin America and the ghettos of Philadelphia during the early and mid-sixties. I did not choose to be challenged and to have my worldview upset. That was a by-product of my curiosity to see the world—as a tourist. Having been challenged, I was then offered an option; either to remain locked into the divisions of my narrow world, or to stand with the oppressed and to seek transformation and oneness.

It is when we choose to exercise the option for unity that we then are faced with the question of how. What are some of the paths to solidarity?

## Being Present

A Spanish woman who has lived and worked in Latin America and the United States is now serving as a prison chaplain in New York State. Standing in the prison visitation line one day, a woman behind her asked, "Are you here to see your son?" The question jolted her. She was there to minister to the prisoners, to be in solidarity with them. But not one of them was her son. That was a different matter altogether.

The image of waiting in line to see her son would not go away, and she began to ask herself what it meant for her, an educated middle-class woman, to be there. "What does it mean for me to be in solidarity? What is solidarity? How much do I want to be here? How much do I want to protect myself?

How far can my connection with this woman go?" She felt the distance between them because of their differing circumstances. It was not her son who was behind the bars.

These were painful but legitimate questions to ask. In asking them she discovered the truth of her circumstance. She knew what the role of chaplain entailed, but she didn't know yet what it meant to be in solidarity. What she did know about solidarity was that it was important to be present—as fully present as she was capable—even before she knew what to do.

If we wait until we've got it all figured out in terms of solidarity, we will spend the rest of our lives cut off and absent from others. Being present does not mean that we have the right agenda or that we understand what must be done. It simply means that we are compelled to stand by the other. It may not make sense, it may not be carefully thought out, but we know that we must be there.

Being present is very difficult for some of us. We have been trained to fix things, set the agenda, solve the problems, do something. But being present often calls for a stillness that many of us have not learned: learning to be in the woods rather than simply walking through them, learning to listen to other cultures rather than merely trying to analyze and explain them, learning to be there for the tears of a loved one rather than just focusing on the problem. There can be no holistic solidarity if we don't learn how to be present, even stumblingly, without full understanding, with nothing apparent to offer.

Perhaps this is what the old hymn has to teach us today—"nothing in my hands I bring, simply to thy cross I cling." There are times when no strategies work, no analysis is adequate, no words are completely truthful, no actions effective. At such moments we can do nothing more than be there for the other.

That is why the story of Ruth is so powerful. Her resolve to go with Naomi was not a plan, it was a willingness to be present. In her presence she became more to Naomi than seven sons. Neither Ruth nor Naomi could anticipate what such a presence would mean. Would they die together there in Judah? Would they live forsaken and lonely lives? Would their support lead to a new beginning? Neither knew, but Ruth knew that she must remain with her mother-in-law, despite the uncertainties. In being present, their journey together began.

In 1983 a group of North Americans who were alarmed over the foreign policy of the United States with regard to Nicaragua were invited by some Nicaraguan evangelical churches to visit and see firsthand what was happening. They discovered that our government was arming an opposition force of "Contras" that was indiscriminately killing women and children as well as soldiers. In addition, U.S. economic policies were ruining the economy through boycott and influencing trade and international loan policies unfavorable to Nicaragua. The force of the United States government was being hurled against a tiny nation of three million people, more than half of whom were under the age of fifteen. Realizing that U.S. foreign policy must be challenged and changed, these persons formed a nationwide movement called Witness for Peace, a central aim of which was to send U.S. citizens to the beleaguered villages of rural Nicaragua to stand with the people.

I went on one of those trips the next year. In a rural town near the Honduran border, where the Contra activity was particularly heavy, a number of large rallies had been held during the previous year by Witness for Peace volunteers. At the rally that day I overheard an old Nicaraguan woman say, "I don't know what these people are doing here, but they do it all the time." Looking back, I'm not sure that we knew what we were doing there either, but at the very least we wanted to demonstrate by our presence that not everyone in the United States wanted to destroy them.

It was through that presence, however unsophisticated it might have been at its inception, that Witness for Peace learned firsthand of the devastation in Nicaragua and emerged as a leading organization in challenging U.S. Central American policy through its documentation, educational, and lobbying efforts. "Being present" was a critical and early step in the process of building solidarity.

Sometimes there is nothing to say or do and all that is left for us is the faithful, undramatic tenacity of Ruth: "Where you go, I will go; your people shall be my people" (Ruth 1:16).

## Telling Our Stories

One of the loveliest people I have ever known was an elderly British widow, Vera Plant. She was eighty-two when I first began staying in her home on my semiannual visits to Sheffield, England, during the 1980s. Vera was a Victorian woman, patrician in bearing, warm and affirming in her manner, and curious to learn all she could about life.

During one of my first visits with her she told me about her own journey. The year before, when she was eighty-one, she was asked whether she would be willing to accommodate a visitor who was coming to study at the Urban Theology Unit. She agreed. When the guest arrived and Vera Plant greeted her at the door, there was a moment of tension and discomfort. Vera was surprised to discover that the visitor was a black woman from Africa. This was the first time Vera had ever been face to face with a black person, and she was startled and unsure of what to do. Her manners won the day, and she invited the woman into her living room where an uneasy conversation began.

The guest began to speak about her homeland and her family. "As she did, something happened," Vera said. "All of a sudden, I realized that she had a mother and father just as I, that she had friends and dreams, just as I, that she was a human being, just as I." In the sharing of her story, the woman became a person and no longer a threat. She stayed with Vera for several months and returned several years later with her husband. From that day, Vera Plant's house became a center of hospitality for all people.

There is a power in sharing our stories that enables us to get beyond seeing the other as merely a representation of our preconceptions and stereotypes, a power that often overcomes our defenses and transcends our limitations. This is especially true when we tell of our sufferings. Much of the Bible's power comes from its stories about the people's struggle to overcome oppression and to find meaning in the face of death and destruction. These stories of suffering range from the most personal, such as Job's, to the larger collective laments of the nation in exile.

We can understand the power of stories to overcome divisions when we reflect on the way in which scripture has spoken to persons of every culture, race, and circumstance, no matter how different they may be. In some ways, there are few cultures and languages as disparate as that of the Hebrew poet's and our technological Western society. We speak and think in functional terms: speed, cost/benefit analysis, balances of power. Yet who can deny the power of the Twenty-third Psalm when it speaks of the Lord as our shepherd who leads us to still waters and comforts us in the valley of the shadow of death. The power of the poem resides in the reverberation that is set up between the experiences it points to and our own experiences. There is a depth in each of us, a depth of the human condition that is touched when we share our stories. And the incredible fact is how similar our stories often are.

The centrality of story in uniting people who have traditionally been divided is clearly visible in several contemporary communities. Much of the power and cohesion of the women's movement has been gained through the use of story. The primary activity of women's consciousness-raising groups has been the sharing of their stories. Many women have attested to their isolation and estrangement from other women. In their consciousness-raising groups many have discovered the similarity of their stories and of their longings. In sharing how their lives are dominated or curtailed or distorted or wounded, a solidarity often occurs that had previously eluded them.

The same has been true among many peasants and urban

poor in Latin America. A common phenomenon of oppression is the failure of the oppressed to work together. Divide and conquer has been an effective strategy used by those in control. The poor in Latin America have been a glaring example of the success of that strategy; traditionally they have been no threat to the status quo. Even many of the so-called revolutions have been merely coups d'état in which the poor have been pawns, not the shapers of the nation's destiny. However, through the rise of base Christian communities the poor have been organizing and now pose a serious threat to the entrenched power of dictators, oligarchies, and the military. One of the most important factors in building solidarity and action has been the opportunity to share their stories and to reflect on the biblical stories that reverberate with their own. They know now that they are not alone.

Perhaps the best known example in this country of the power of story to build solidarity among the divided is that of Alcoholics Anonymous. There, persons who have hidden the truth from others and themselves bring their own stories to light and in doing so discover their own truth and find the power that comes in knowing that one is part of a larger struggle. These and other experiences underscore that there can be no solidarity for those who are out of touch with their own story. Without that, there is nothing to share, no basis for trust and connection.

Sharing our stories, however, will not overcome all divisions in a single blow. The suspicions run too deep, the problems of communication present hurdles that loom large before us, and our tendency to self-preoccupation is not easily given up. Nor does sharing our stories overcome all differences. We may still find ourselves disagreeing about what is to be done, even when we discover that we share the same fundamental human condition. Culture, strategies, and styles may lead to a variety of responses. Sharing our stories does provide us with a foundation for solidarity.

Not only is story a critical component in building solidarity, it also helps to overcome the purely functional approach to solidarity that is often the case with political alliances. It is far more difficult to treat the other as simply a convenient and temporary ally for the sake of a common goal when we know their story. When we share our stories we touch each other's souls. We are intimately connected, not merely functionally aligned. We tread on holy ground that has the power to unite us as friends.

But a word of caution must be raised here. It is not easy to share our stories, especially when we have had our identities and powers wrested from us. In telling our own story we are recovering a stolen identity and that can be painful and terrifying. There are parts of our story that we may wish to keep buried, even from ourselves. We make ourselves uncomfortably vulnerable when we share our story with others, for we no longer can hide behind the stereotypes and posturing.

I remember an African American whom I found fearsome in his anger and attitude. I was so intimidated by him that it was impossible for me to be authentic around him. I kept trying to figure out what I should say and do in order to gain his approval. It came as quite a shock to discover that he, too, was afraid. He was not the totally secure, confident, all-together person I had imagined him to be. With that discovery his power *over* me was destroyed. What took its place was a power *with* as we discovered a shared journey and task. The danger, of course, was that in sharing his fears with me I was now in a position to take advantage of his vulnerability and exercise power over him. Unless we become mutually vulnerable, such sharing can result in new domination.

There is another barrier to sharing our stories. Several years ago I taught a weekly seminar on solidarity and liberation. There were six of us, women and men: Euro-American, African American and Hispanic. Our approach included sharing our experiences of alienation and struggles for liberation. I had assumed that such sharing would provide a common base for our work together. The thing that astounded us all was the unexpected difficulty we experienced in sharing and hearing each other. It was as if all the old fears, stereotypes, and blocks were there with a vengeance. One of the members seemed afraid that if too much power were granted the other person's story it would diminish the power of his own. The struggle to move to a deeper level of solidarity was enormous. If it was that way with that group of committed people, then we should not be surprised to discover the same dynamic elsewhere.

In that experience is revealed one of the fundamental barriers to building solidarity: a hierarchy of oppression. There is a danger of creating a hierarchy of alienation and oppression and thereby delegitimizing the power of those whose stories seem less severe. Certainly some kinds of pain are far more severe than others, and we must set priorities in terms of the use of resources, the order of addressing various pains, and so on. That is far different, however, from dismissing the other's pain as either unreal or unimportant. Pain is pain, alienation is alienation, oppression is oppression. Only when we move beyond competition at the level of sharing our stories of alienation and suffering is there hope that we can stand together to do what is necessary to minimize or alleviate the suffering of all. If those who have been struggling for liberation find it difficult to hear the other's story, how much more so for those who are at the point of beginning to struggle.

The stories to be shared are not only those of suffering, however. There are also stories in which we share our dreams and hopes.

The creation narrative in Genesis reveals the power in sharing our dreams, our hopes, our imaginings. God shared a longing: "Let us make. . . ." God longed for a world, for beauty, for companionship. So God shared those deepest longings and, in speaking those words, transformed the darkness into light, the formlessness into beauty, and the emptiness into abundance.

The Bible is, above all else, the story of longing, the sharing of God's dreams, first for companionship and then for restoration of a lost relationship. When John speaks of the Word being made flesh and dwelling among us, that is God's way of sharing the dream and longing for restoration. The Word is shared and in the sharing we are drawn to the one who speaks. Solidarity is made possible by the sharing of our longings.

There appear to be almost insurmountable obstacles to sharing our stories. Our fears dominate us. We speak different languages, not only linguistically different languages such as Spanish, Korean, and English but also the languages that arise from male and female cultures, from artistic and technical orientations, from differences in temperament, and so on. And we are such a noisy and busy culture that there is little space for our stories to be told and heard. Not only are we constantly on the go, but even those places that might provide space, such as in corporate worship, are filled with noise and activity. The silence that precedes sharing is a rarity. Our programmatic, problem-solving orientation leaves little room for listening and sharing.

The awful danger of not knowing each other's stories is that we fail to build genuine friendships—caring relationships—that can shape and guide our actions. In the absence of friendship our solidarity is a temporary convenience for the sake of the accomplishment of a specific task, and we are tempted to reduce everything and everyone to their instrumental function. Without friendship as a basis for solidarity we lack the fullness to which the reign of God points. In God's reign, it is not only armies that are conquered, but tears that are wiped away, not only new economic forms that are created, but friendships and families that are born.

Sharing our stories not only serves to create solidarity, it also gives solidarity a human face.

## Identifying a Common Enemy

I have visited Cuba on two occasions, once in 1967 and once in 1987. Many things changed during those twenty years, but one thing remained remarkably constant, namely the Cubans' identification of a common enemy. It has been suggested by many political analysts that if the United States had not continuously provided reasons for Cuba to hate our government, Castro would not have the solid, almost worshipful, backing that he has enjoyed over the years. While that is too limited a reading of the basis of Castro's power, there is much truth in it. Our aggressive military actions, economic blockades, trade embargoes, and attempts to discredit Cuba through the international press have given the people an enemy that they can all hate, and this has helped to solidify their resistance and resolve.

This has produced a remarkable internal political stability in Cuba. There are dissidents, of course, and tales of political prisoners. But there has been relatively little expression of discontent among the common people. This can be attributed to many factors, including a fairly tight system of local policing and surveillance. It is also true that the citizenry of Cuba is the most heavily armed in the hemisphere. Almost everyone has a gun. Despite this, there have been no attempts to assassinate Castro or overthrow the government. Castro has effectively used the specter of U.S. imperialism to bring the people together. It has worked for the people of Cuba to have a common enemy.

We have used this same strategy in our country. Dissenters have often been accused of being communists. Under the banner of national security we have stirred up patriotic fervor by appealing to the people's fears of the great beast from Russia. Anticommunism reached its zenith of paranoia during the McCarthy era of the early fifties, but it continued to be a major ploy in the suppression of dissent and the whipping up of patriotic frenzy until the dramatic changes in the Soviet Union and Eastern Europe in the late '80s and early '90s. Even now, the specter of the revival of communism is held over us, and Third World liberation movements are uniformly branded as communist, whether they are or not.

Similarly, white supremacists have used many people's fear of African Americans to build their ranks. Historically, having a common enemy has been an effective tactic in building solidarity, either in support of the status quo or in support of transformation. Sadly, however, there has been a rather startling inability during the last thirty to forty years among more progressive religious and political groups within our country to agree upon a common enemy. Each group has had a different primary enemy. For many African Americans it has been Euro-Americans; for many women it has been men; for many Hispanics it has been Anglos; for many poor it has been capitalists; and so on. In far too many cases this disagreement has been characterized by more than simply claiming one of these as the primary enemy; often there has been an insistence that the enemy, as they perceive it, is the only important enemy. The most oppressed groups in our society have often been at odds over identification of the enemy. In the absence of agreement, the basis for solidarity has been rather shaky.

At first, talk of an enemy makes most of us uncomfortable. It openly acknowledges conflict, which we have been taught to avoid. Further, the presence of an enemy suggests that we have failed, that we have done something wrong. If we had just loved more, understood the other better, or were more effective in our responses, there would be no enemy. We have been taught that we are to be a peaceful people. Enemies have no place in our scheme of things.

Even when we recognize the presence of an enemy, many of us are reluctant to judge, let alone to form solidarity on the basis of it. What right do we have to judge, to think of people in terms of "enemy"? We know that all of us are somehow implicated in evil, so we are reticent to set ourselves up as the judges of others. We know too well the temptation to reduce the enemy to total evil. We know our history too well to be so easily duped by self-righteousness. The Crusades, the Inquisition, Jonestown, fallen TV evangelists, and our own feet of clay, cause us to hesitate when someone speaks of our having an enemy. Immediately someone quotes Matthew 7:1, "Judge not, that you be not judged."

This use of the biblical text is completely inappropriate. Elsewhere in the scriptures we are told that we must test the spirits (1 John 4:1) and warned that we are engaged in a battle. The admonition to avoid judging others needs to be understood for what it intended. It was a call to modesty and humility. Jesus was quoting a common Jewish aphorism that was meant to caution people against self-righteousness. We should know that not only do we judge, but we stand before

God who judges us. Do not judge without recognizing that you, too, stand under judgment. Never did he mean to suggest that we should remove ourselves from making judgments about right and wrong, good and evil, appropriate and inappropriate. It is undeniably clear from scripture that we have enemies, and we are in a battle against all that destroys life. As Jesus pointed out, we are not to avoid having enemies—they come with the territory—we are to love them.

Identifying the enemy is one of the important tasks of the church. We are called upon to do this when we explore the nature of sin and when we test the spirits. Such exploration and testing necessarily involve us in careful social analysis, a task that demands the participation of the entire community. It is here that theory and critical thinking become part of the faithful response of the worshiping community. Identifying and understanding the enemy should be an integral part of the educational ministry—including sermons—of our congregations and our judicatories. So long as we are content to generalize about sin and injustice we will remain as Don Quixotes, tilting at windmills, feeling good that we are doing something, but changing nothing.

Identifying the enemy involves us in a task that demands the greatest specificity. Only a false unity can be derived from a general denunciation of evil. This is an insidious dynamic within our churches and largely accounts for how it is that people who are fundamentally committed to opposite goals can often seem to agree about essentials of the faith. Oppressors and oppressed can only exist side by side in church when they have failed to be specific about the nature of the evil present among them. As long as injustice is denounced abstractly, everyone can join in, from former President Reagan to the widow whose husband and infant were killed by the Contras, from Leona Helmsley to the homeless elderly on the street outside one of her ostentatious hotels. Once the evil is identified by name, then those who are caught in the contradictions of our world and who function as oppressors may be able to question their lives and begin the rather tentative journey toward unity. Even with that, divisions will still exist, but a concrete step toward unity will have been taken. True solidarity begins with an agreed-upon, specific recognition of the enemy.

As I have written elsewhere, this specific reading of the signs of the times, or testing of the spirits, is what can and should happen in the church's ritual of confession as well as in our educational endeavors.[1] When we change our ritual of confession from an amorphous litany to a carefully articulated denunciation of specific evils and failures, we will have made a start toward genuine unity.

One of the most encouraging developments in contemporary liberation theology is the increasing recognition of the interrelatedness of the principalities and powers against which we struggle. Racism, patriarchy, and capitalism are often now understood to be part of the same fabric, its warp and woof. The enemy is more complex than many had imagined, and hence the struggle is more complex. Perhaps the appeal of the single-enemy theory was its simplicity; but it is an appeal that ultimately leads us to failure in our struggle. In many ways we are at the dawn of a new era in social analysis with the recognition that the enemy facing each of us is the enemy facing all of us.[2]

In some ways the biblical notion of evil seems to recognize this complexity when it distinguishes between the manifestations of evil, such as pride, envy, greed, and lust, and the fundamental source of evil, which is idolatry—the worshiping of a false god. The principalities and powers that operate in the cosmos are understood as either good or evil, depending upon whom they serve. And specific actors are judged on the basis of the God they serve. Persons whose ultimate commitment is to national security, personal privilege, or tranquility will find that they are serving the god of oppression, no matter how fine they may be as individuals. While the actors and actions may vary, what links them is their common idolatrousness—serving the god of oppression and death.

It is important to distinguish between the common enemy and strategic enemies. Too often we miss the forest for the trees when it comes to this. We face a common enemy, the interwoven structure of oppression as it functions today. At different times in history the common enemy has different shapes, so it becomes critical to identify its contemporary form. I have suggested that it is the interrelated forms of racism, capitalism, and patriarchy that together form the face of the common enemy today. It is these, in concert with one another, that cause poverty, nuclear threat, ecological destruction, homophobia, abuse, ageism, genocide, and the myriad other forms of oppression that characterize life for modern society.

Our multifaceted common enemy has its legions, those who carry out its dreadful aims, those who keep the structures intact. One may find them in various positions of authority: politicians, bureaucrats, preachers, writers, investors, generals. These are our strategic enemies. They are not our enemies—as persons—but as they fulfill their ungodly tasks they become our strategic enemies. It is still possible to love them, just as Jesus pleaded for forgiveness for his executioners and tormentors, realizing that they did not know what they were doing. Jesus understood that they were caught in the web of evil and as servants of that evil were guilty, but as children of God they deserved forgiveness. They were not his eternal enemies to be defeated, but his brothers and sisters who needed saving. The ultimate act of love toward our enemies is to fight against the evil they are upholding, for then we are fighting for the salvation of all of us, for the restoration of their lost humanity as well as our own.

Since the common enemy of our time is the interrelated structure of capitalism, patriarchy and racism, the complexity and insidiousness of its form makes it difficult to sort out who our strategic enemies are and just where we can do battle. Many of our strategic enemies are good people. It is not only Machiavellian manipulators who support the common enemy—often it is people of good will who are unwilling to recognize, name, or resist the evil that they are serving. Like co-dependents, they are unwilling to name that which is destroying them and others. Sometimes the fears that have been produced by the common enemy—fear of unemployment, or rejection, or war, or loss of privilege—cause very ordinary people to become conservators of the old arrangements even though they ultimately stand to lose. Our strategic enemies are as often our neighbors as they are the infamous: Oliver North, David Duke, or P. W. Botha.

In the United States the "ordinariness" of the strategic enemy is often advanced by a confusing theory of class. Most of us are taught that we are members of the middle class, thereby making us somehow distinct from the working class and the underclass of the unemployed, persons on welfare, and the institutionalized. Such an understanding is fundamentally wrong. When class is understood in terms of power—power over our work and power to decide for the common good—we soon discover that these decisions do not rest in our hands but in the hands of those who control the basic economy and, thereby, the political structures. Think of how years of popular struggle and even laws against support of the Contras did not stand in the way of those leaders who wanted to oppose the Sandinistas in Nicaragua. Or note how most middle class folks have little or no say over whether their office or plant will shut down, or move, or lay off personnel. We simply wait for the axe to fall. Such decisions are beyond our influence most of the time.

The truth is that the principal difference between the so-called middle class and the lower class, in terms of power, lies in the power to consume. We have been granted the privilege of consuming more, thereby firing the ovens of capitalism and at the same time anesthetizing ourselves from the pain of alienation. This reality cuts across gender and race lines and is then compounded when the dynamics of sexism and racism are also present. When we buy the myth of the middle class, we become one of the strategic enemies ourselves.

Even when our strategic enemies are serving the cause of evil unwittingly, we are called to stand against them in a way that offers the chance for their redemption as well as ours.

What has tended to separate many of us who are struggling for liberation is the specificity of our strategic enemies. For the oppressed majority in South Africa the strategic enemies are the Afrikaners who seek to maintain their destructive power at all costs. For the abused wife the strategic enemy is her husband. For the unemployed miner in Appalachia it is the industry and the particular company that fired him or her. The nature of our strategic enemies calls for specific responses on our part. This calls for distinctions among us. What can unite us is the realization that we all face a common enemy. While our strategic enemies may differ and call for distinctive responses, it is essential that we recognize the common enemy that destroys us all: the interrelated forces of contemporary Western civilization—racism, capitalism, and patriarchy.

## Worship

Implicit and explicit in what I have suggested about paths to unity is the dynamic of worship. One of the most distinctive contributions to solidarity that the church, synagogue, or mosque can make is through its worship, in which the dimensions of friendship and politics are present and fostered—or at least can be. In a summary manner let me identify the ways in which worship can contribute to solidarity.

In worship we give recognition to the source of our unity. We all stand before God our creator in whose image we have been made. From beginning to end we are reminded to "kneel before the Lord our maker," that it is God "from whom all blessings flow" and that we are all God's handiwork. The call to worship roots us in our source. It sets our lives within the larger cosmic context that we so easily forget at other times. Our failure to recognize the cosmic nature of what is at stake often reduces us to isolated individuals competing for crumbs, willing to sacrifice anything and anyone in the process. When we know that we are part of a cosmic struggle, the ante is upped.

In worship we give recognition to the power that makes possible our unity in the face of insurmountable obstacles, namely, the Spirit of God at work among us. In worship we give recognition to our kinship: that we are sisters and brothers. In worship we name the forces of evil against which God and we struggle. In worship we acknowledge our complicity and the common lot we bear with all others, including those whom we call enemies. In worship, through scripture and sermon, we hear the stories of those who have gone before as they bear witness to God's power and their struggle for liberation in the face of evil. In specifically Christian worship we participate in baptism, which calls us to disciplined obedience in the community, and in the Eucharist, by which we commit ourselves to share in the sufferings of the world in the same manner that Jesus suffered for us. In worship we offer our gifts as thanksgiving and pledge that we shall put them at the disposal of all those in need.

Or at least that is what worship *can* be about. But as I have indicated, too often this is not the case. Too often the church becomes the place in which co-dependency, denial, escape, and ignorance are fostered. It is not my intent here to delineate further the failures of our churches to nurture solidarity. It is important, however, to deliberately view our formal worship life as a critical aspect of the path to solidarity. Presence, sharing our stories, and identifying a common enemy are all part of the life of an authentic worshiping community.

It is tempting simply to say that we should break down the artificial class, gender, and racial barriers that shape our congregations so that a more genuinely diverse mix would be present at and take part in the leadership of worship. But it is precisely because we have not taken necessary preliminary steps that this condition prevails, and all our righteous challenges to the ecclesiastical status quo will do little to change things. What we need now are some ways of being that will move us beyond tokenism and toward being a gathered community that truly embraces the differences among us.

Beginning where most of us are, our churches, mosques, and synagogues could help us get in touch with our own stories. Small groups that provide a safe space for sharing, that model ways of getting in touch, that provide encouragement and support are a good beginning. We could utilize many of the discoveries that have grown out of the various approaches to group therapy from Gestalt, to twelve-step, to women's consciousness-raising, to the Latin American base communities. Absolutely constitutive of this approach would be worship: the sharing of the scriptures that give witness to the similar struggles of others, moving us beyond the parochial frame of reference of our own experience or that of our own small group into the groaning of prayer in which we share our deepest longings and fears.

Also, these small groups could be enabled to go the next step, which is to connect their own stories with the biblical stories and with those of others beyond the walls of our common relationships. Once we begin to connect our stories with those beyond our experience, our immediate community and our nation, what was once thought to be individual becomes political, that is, connected with the *polis.*

Elsewhere I have spoken of the role of prayer as the sharing of our fears and our longings.[3] I am absolutely convinced that a recovery of aspects of the traditional prayer meeting is critical for a worshiping community to become a community of solidarity. I say "aspects," as I realize that forms of prayer will necessarily be different for different persons and communities, and we cannot force people into molds that do not fit them. If our deepest longings are to emerge naturally, the context must be one that fits us, not forces us. Prayer meetings in this sense should be an invitation, not a format.

In worship we acknowledge the source of our unity and our strength. In worship we share our own dreams, our joys, and our concerns through music, prayer, the sermon, the confession, the sacraments. In worship we weep with Jesus and our brothers and sisters over the city, over the world. In worship we understand ourselves to be one, we identify with those with whom we kneel. In worship we commit ourselves to act on behalf of the outcast, the imprisoned, the hungry, and the sick.

## Engagement in Common Action

According to the Gospel of Matthew, chapter 25, when the final judgment takes place people will be divided, right and left, heaven and hell, blessing and torment. And we will be surprised by the basis of the judgment. Jesus will recognize, as his own, those who gave food to the hungry, a cup of cold water to the thirsty, hospitality to the stranger, clothing to the naked, and visited the sick and the imprisoned.

The willingness of Jesus to invite us into his home—to unite us with him—is based upon our actions of solidarity. There can finally be no solidarity without action. We may say the right things, think the right thoughts, make the right appearance, worship together, and even denounce the same enemy, but until we act in concert—until we work together for the transformation of the circumstances of oppression—we have not contributed to solidarity. At the end of the day, if we have not engaged in actions for solidarity when the opportunities presented themselves, nothing else counts.

I proposed earlier that in sharing our stories it is counterproductive to assign a hierarchy of reality to the oppression and suffering that is being shared. There will be no basis for solidarity unless we are able to accept the fact that one person's experience of oppression is just as real as anyone else's.

While there is no hierarchy of reality when it comes to oppression, there is almost always a hierarchy of action. Most of us would consider it our first order of business to intervene in a situation where a life is at stake. Other forms of threat or oppression, however equally real, would take second place.

In some cases, setting priorities in the face of equally real forms of oppression is relatively clear and noncontroversial. In a world in which the systematic destruction of life is so rampant, however, things become confusingly complex. Do we turn our attention to the starving in Africa, the peasants of Nicaragua being crushed by the Contras, the bloodletting in the Middle East, the African American infants in our own country whose mortality rate is worse than that of infants in many Third World countries, the ecological threat that hovers over the entire planet, the horrible wasteland of our state and local prisons, or the majority in South Africa who are systematically disenfranchised, imprisoned, and killed? The complexity and enormity of the demands has left many of us guilt-ridden and paralyzed.

One of my colleagues has a sign tacked on her bookshelf. It is the definition of the word "triority." A triority is "three things that absolutely must be done first." This is where the rubber hits the road—there is no escaping the difficulties we face at the action stage of solidarity. The various needs are both legitimate and overwhelming, and the available resources are so few. But we must act, lest our deepest wishes and highest ideals remain powerless to transform our world.

How do we decide where to cast our lot? How do we decide where to use our limited resources in the face of such overwhelming needs? There is no formula to ease the pain of this dilemma. There are no easy answers, but there are some clues.

At a certain level the decision is given to us; it comes with the territory. Certain events touch our lives, certain people cross our path, certain experiences make us more empathic to one issue or the other. Living in Northern cities has thrust the reality of racism upon me in a way that I cannot ignore. My travels in Latin America that began out of idle curiosity have led me into concerns for the people of that region of the world. Conversely, I am aware of the tragedy of the Middle East, yet the reality is that I spend far less time reading about, worrying about, and working for transformation there. The phrase "bloom where you are planted" might be an appropriate one when it comes to solidarity. The circumstances of life have led us each to be where we are. These are the people to whom God has given us and, in most cases, it is here where we are to begin—with the context we've inherited.

There are potential problems with this. Certain contexts deserve to be abandoned—like dust to be shaken off our feet—because the people with whom we relate there are consistently unwilling to wrestle with the gospel of transformation. And there is certainly the danger that our context, however open to transformation, may simply be too con-

stricted. When all of the stories are similar, the basis for transformation is too narrow. In that case, we must find ways to
expand our context to include the voices and lives that can
challenge us. I suggest that under most circumstances, when
it comes to deciding the action priorities, they be ones that are
related to the experiences of our "world."

However, these decisions must be made in community. It is
not our right to decide alone, especially as individuals whose
backgrounds are privileged relative to those with whom we
seek to be in solidarity. We dare not trust simply our own
instincts and experiences to be our guide. It is here that a
community is so critical.

But it is not just any community that is to be trusted with
shaping decisions about priorities and actions. It certainly cannot be a community limited to persons of privilege, even if
those persons are seeking solidarity with the dispossessed.
Having come to the decision that solidarity is the only way
toward unity, there is no possibility for authentically estab-
lishing the priorities and boundaries for action except with
those who are without privilege. We must open ourselves to
them.

There are a variety of ways that this can occur, only one of
which is through direct conversation. Sometimes victims don't
want to talk to you, especially if you are of the group that has
caused their victimization. That was true in Detroit as we ran
from the youths who were hurling stones at us. It is often
counterproductive to try to force our presence and ask for
dialogue.

Even when no one wants you present at their meetings or
cares to engage you in discussion or planning, it is possible to
hear, to learn what their hearts yearn for. It is possible to hear
the stories that they have taken the trouble to share: by reading the literature that comes out of their struggle, by listening
to the music that reflects the fears and hopes of their world,
by viewing the art that reveals their truth. Any of us who
claim to want solidarity but find ourselves without clues
should begin by examining what we read, what we watch,
what we listen to. We have no excuse for not knowing the

stories of the dispossessed. And their stories provide us with clues for our actions.

Under certain circumstances there might be only one choice for the focus of one's energies and of the alliances one makes, as seems to be the case for struggle in contemporary South Africa. In contrast, there is not just one choice for us in the United States when it comes to being in solidarity. Racism, classism, homophobia, sexism, ageism, militarism, international imperialism, ecological destruction, and other forms of the demonic all legitimately demand our response. The multifacetedness of our common enemy poses enormous problems for us.

The complexity of choosing action priorities is present even among the most overtly oppressed. For example, many African American women have rejected the feminist movement as primarily or exclusively addressing issues of Euro-American middle-class women and as being essentially racist.[4] Nonetheless, this does not mean that they have not understood that their own oppression has involved not only racism and classism but also sexism. Much contemporary literature written by African American women points to this complex triple jeopardy and recognizes sexism as part of their oppression. They have adopted a new name for themselves—"womanist"—in order to affirm this recognition and to distinguish themselves from feminists. In our society, decisions about alliances and actions are not necessarily immediately clear and never simple.

The multifaceted dimensions of our alienation and the magnitude of the task demand community, not only to guide us in setting priorities but also to address the many aspects that must be battled. We are waging a war on many fronts, and it is impossible for any one person or any group to fight successfully on all these fronts at one time. We need the gifts and understanding of each other in order to engage in the struggle simultaneously. We must fight as if our particular battle were the most crucial one of the war, but we must be wise enough and modest enough to know that others are doing the same in their arena. God has given us gifts, temperaments, and

personal histories that best suit us for battle at a specific location at a specific time. We need each other.

The question of who should decide the course of action to
transform the world always comes up, often raised by those
of us who are used to running the show. What does solidarity
imply in terms of decision-making? First, we need to avoid
processes of decision-making that are geared to maintaining
the old order. An example of such a process is *Robert's Rules of
Order.* These parliamentary rules have served a very important
purpose in the democratic process, such as providing guidelines and protection and ensuring proper debate procedures.
However, they seem to work best for those who plan ahead,
who feel comfortable verbalizing in public, and who enjoy
debating.

Because of this, it is not uncommon to experience well-
planned and orchestrated "railroading" in many meetings. I
have used such skills myself on more than one occasion to
achieve what I believed to be a correct outcome, and I have
been snookered on other occasions by similarly clever players
of the parliamentary game.

But these parliamentary processes often make it difficult for
people who function more spontaneously, for those who are
intuitive, for those who are introverts, for those functioning
in a second language, for those who have never believed that
they had anything worth saying. If we were to expand our
decision-making process to include praying, eating, informal
sharing, and a more informal meeting style we might discover
a larger and different group of people participating. Generally,
these would be persons who have been held speechless by the
dominant structures of power.

The second issue is majority rule. I'm not convinced that
majority rule should be the sacred idol that we have made
it, especially among groups of people who are trying to be
in solidarity. It is quite a different matter when it comes to
nation-states. We have seen the manner in which a small
minority can dominate, resulting in the marginalization of the
majority, as in South Africa or Poland, making majority rule

desirable. But, among marginal groups themselves, as they struggle against the dominant forces of society, something different may be appropriate.

This recognition was at the heart of the corrective that developed among movement groups in the '60s and early '70s, when they adopted decision by consensus. Consensus, of course, can also be a tedious and even manipulative process. There is no single formula for decision-making among those wishing to be in solidarity, but at the very least friendship would suggest that issues of importance cannot be settled simply by the majority.

A process of careful hearing, sensing, and even reversing decisions needs to be possible. Consensus is not always the best way, but I'm convinced that those who moved in this direction were in touch with something that we need to explore further. If solidarity means politics and friendship, then perhaps it is worth a try.

Lastly, since the decision-making and action stage of solidarity inevitably involves us in compromises, we cannot avoid the need for confession. We cannot live with compromise without having rituals for confession. That is, we cannot neglect confession if we wish to avoid capitulation to callousness and self-righteousness.

Imagine how different church would be if our confessions were characterized by acknowledgment of the failures we had experienced while seeking justice and liberation, rather than the innocuous breast-beating in which most of us engage as we speak of our complicity or failure to act at all. At the very least, our sins would not be so boringly repetitive.

Unity as solidarity in the struggle for liberation is a unity that includes political action and friendship. It is holistic. Authentic solidarity is based on our longings for the unity that has too long been denied us and upon the strategic understanding that transformation cannot occur as long as we are divided. Solidarity demands that we build trust through the mutual hope and vulnerability that come with sharing our stories. It asks that we be present, even when we don't know

ate destruction of all who were in Sodom and Gomorrah when Abraham pled on behalf of Lot and his family. To speak of God and humans as friends is to open up the possibility of mutuality. It is to understand prayer as more than asking but rather as the sharing of longings; the longings of God and the longings of our hearts. And the longings we share are for the transformation of our lives and world.

When Jesus wishes to reveal the essence of the relationship between himself and his disciples, he calls them friends. (See John 15.) No longer are they servants, simply doing the master's bidding, but now they stand together, sharing the same longings. The depth of his friendship is so great that he is willing to lay down his life for his followers.

To be in solidarity is an act of love. And to love is to be vulnerable enough to share needs as well as resources. It is to share even when the sharing isn't equal. It may even require laying down one's life. As long as there is mutual sharing and vulnerability, the alliance holds.

Sallie McFague offers the image of friends not standing simply face to face but as standing side by side, facing a common task or interest. This image allows friendship and politics to be linked because it moves us beyond the merely sentimental or romantic notion of friendship as two people simply wrapped up in one another. They not only have one another, they have a shared vision and purpose.

McFague describes God as friend, as one who covenants, supports, and cares for us out of loving choice. And we are God's friends, standing side by side with God in the task of caring for the world.[9] One of the reasons it is so important for us to understand the friendship dimension of solidarity is that when solidarity is understood simply as politics there is a temptation to assume a "control mode"—to think that all that is at stake is achievement and that the basis for all decisions is effectiveness. It is, however, precisely the attempt to control life and history that has gotten us into the state we are in. If it is inappropriate to think of God as the sovereign one who controls history, it is equally fallacious to think of humans as the controllers of our destiny. Control is not the mode of

what to do. It involves disciplined analysis that enables us to name the enemy. It means recognizing the source of our strength through worship. And it calls us to the risks of action, with all the limits and compromises that attend our way. These are at least some of the paths to solidarity.

The question for many of us is whether there is room for us on that path. Is solidarity a reality that can be experienced only by certain groups, or is it open to all who would venture on the journey? For many, this question becomes a burning issue of identity and calling. We turn next to this question.

# For Reflection

1.  Why is it uncomfortable and painful for the privileged to take part in the struggle for solidarity? Have you ever been stigmatized because of your station in life? Do you feel personal guilt and complicity in the oppression of others?

2.  We can be present with others even when we lack answers and agendas. Can you think of occasions when you have reached out to another person merely by your presence? Do you find it frightening to be in a position of powerlessness?

3.  Have you experienced sorrows and disappointments that you have never shared with others? What things about yourself would you find it difficult to share with a trusted friend? Which is more compelling: the risk of vulnerability or the possible healing of openness?

4.  Have you ever changed your opinion of a person after hearing them tell of some sorrow or suffering?

5.  Have you considered the Bible as the story of God's disappointments and longings? What does it mean to say that Jesus came to share God's story? Does such openness always involve risk?

6.  Do you feel that our culture is too busy and noisy? How often do you experience silence? Are you uncomfortable "doing nothing"?

7. How is it possible for decent people to serve indecent causes? Have you seen this firsthand? Is it possible to love our enemies even while we are fighting against the roles they play?
8. In your religious community are small groups available for intimate sharing? Why are small groups more conducive to honest sharing than large groups?
9. Granting that one person cannot attack every injustice, which needs most demand your involvement? Are you led in this direction by your gifts? Your experiences? Your life situation? How can we pursue our personal callings while safeguarding against parochialism and a narrow worldview?
10. Do you study the literature, art, or music of oppressed people? Do you think exposure to the stories of others can expand your understanding of the victimized?

# For Further Discussion

1. What are the "givens" of your birth and background? How many of these have been advantages and how many disadvantages? What choices have you made that move you toward solidarity? In what way do advantages of birth or position make solidarity more difficult to achieve?
2. Do you feel you have had opportunities to share your story? In what settings? What obstacles have you encountered in allowing others to know you deeply? Is it easier to talk about past disappointments, or future dreams and hopes?
3. Do you think oppressed people have more opportunities to share their stories than do privileged persons? Do Euro-American males also need to reclaim lost identities and names?
4. Are you cheating others when you refuse to share your story? What about when you refuse to listen to another's story?

5.  What is your gut reaction to the desirability of naming a common enemy? Do you think the Jewish prophets pointed to a common enemy? Did Jesus do this? What name do you give to solidarity's common enemy? In what ways should the church undertake to identify the enemy?

6.  "The fundamental source of evil . . . is idolatry—the worshiping of a false god." How does idolatry manifest itself as racism? As patriarchy? As capitalism? Can you think of divisions and oppressions which do not derive from idolatry?

7.  What is the difference between the "common enemy" and "strategic enemies"?

8.  Do you believe that people of privilege and power are also victimized by the system? If so, why do they tend to defend the status quo? What is the real difference between the so-called middle and lower classes?

9.  In your own experience, how fully does worship live up to its potential for reconciliation and empowerment? In what ways does worship fall short? What changes in worship would you encourage?

10. What does it mean to connect our own stories with the biblical stories? How can we facilitate this connection?

# 5
## *What's a Nice Boy Like You Doing in a Place Like This?*

U nder the best of circumstances, the development of solidarity is a slow and painful process. We have already noted many of the factors that prevent unity. Each of the groups that desires to forge alliances for the sake of transformation has its own peculiar dynamics and faces its own set of problems in the attempt. African American women and Euro-American women have been slow to come together in the liberation struggle due to the dynamics created by racism and the roles of men in their respective communities. The different histories experienced by Korean immigrants and African Americans has made understanding and cooperation almost impossible. Korean immigrants have largely come from the middle class; African Americans are the inheritors of slavery and three hundred years of a particular form of racism. Consequently, it has been far easier for Koreans to believe in new possibilities. Many Latinos have found language to be a barrier when trying to forge alliances. These and other instances are evidence of the difficulty and fragility of the path toward solidarity among the oppressed.

Despite the obstacles, many of those who have been outside the circles of power and who have been the victims of oppression have come to understand the necessity of unity for the sake of survival and struggle. Because they understand the necessity for solidarity, sometimes African Americans, Hispanics, women, Native Americans, and Third World persons have worked with groups other than their own toward a common agenda. Theology in the Americas was such a movement. Regardless of the inherent difficulties and infrequency of success, there has been some openness by diverse groups to exploring solidarity. It is far less common, however, to find Euro-American males included with any seriousness in that exploration.

As Theology in the Americas took shape, the role and presence of African Americans, Hispanics, women, and Native Americans became increasingly focused and important. Each of these groups had a distinctly identifiable character and task, and out of the security of their specific identity they found ways to build solidarity. However, many of the Euro-American men found themselves uncertain about their role and questioned the legitimacy or authenticity of their existence as a separate group within the network. They did not become a separate group out of desire, but because there was nowhere else for them to go. The other groups' self-definitions simply did not allow for their inclusion. I was part of the process of defining a Euro-American male group.

The confusion this caused can be seen in the name we selected: The Theologians' Project. One of the problems with this title was that all the other projects included theologians as well. What did this say about the African American, feminist, Hispanic, and Native American theologians? Also, to name ourselves according to our function meant that we defined ourselves according to a completely different criterion than that used by the other groups. They were defined by their accountability to a particular oppressed community. We defined ourselves by our profession. We were there because we wanted to be in solidarity, but neither we nor the others in Theology in the Americas were able to find a way to understand who we were in terms that linked us with the others.

This is a familiar experience for many Euro-American men

today, but its familiarity does not make it any easier. What is their role, if any, in the struggle for liberation?

If we listen to the voices of the oppressed, the fundamental arena of action for Euro-American males needs to be within their own communities. It is a Euro-American male-dominated culture that has sustained the divisions by reelecting officials who will do the will of the power brokers. It is a Euro-American male-dominated culture that has continued to espouse ideas of racial and gender inferiority, nationalism, class myths, homophobia, and other divisive illusions through teaching, writing, entertainment, and preaching. It is a Euro-American male-dominated culture that has drawn ill-gotten benefits from domestic and international economies of oppression. If there is one thing that is clear, it is that Euro-American men are called to struggle for liberation by working to transform others like themselves.

This is not an easy word to hear. In challenging Euro-American men, rejection is to be expected. There is no honor, no glory, and no recognition in such a challenge. I have lost friends, a job, and opportunities in this struggle. Others have lost far more. But these are the people to whom God has given me, and if persons from within this group do not speak out, who will? I may not have much success, but that is not the primary issue. Faithfulness is. This is where I and like-minded Euro-American males are called to take our stand.

In all of our struggles there is much at stake, for the answer is inextricably linked with our sense of what it means to be a human being and what it means to be a Christian. There is also much at stake for the oppressed with whom we wish to be in solidarity, because given the complexity of oppression, friendships and alliances must be carefully chosen and nurtured. The oppressed can ill afford to fall for false promises and glibly trust anyone who claims to be on their side. For all of us this is a question of both identity and vocation.

Several years ago in sharing some personal feelings with a friend, I disclosed that I felt essentially homeless. Rather incredulously, he replied, "I thought you white boys were at home everywhere!" I suppose that I was just as surprised by his response as he was by my confession. I knew that what I was feeling was real, but his response caused me to reflect further on my feelings.

Many Euro-American males feel homeless. (Here I do not mean without shelter. That is the plight of those whom we call the homeless, but their plight is far more serious than simply a lack of shelter. In many cases it also involves a lack of safety, affirmation, or belonging. To be homeless may involve the issue of shelter, but it is far more complex than simply shelter.) It may be difficult for others to accept or even understand that Euro-American males might experience the feeling of homelessness, but it is sometimes the case. While it is true that they can go almost anywhere they choose, this does not mean that they are at home in these places. It is possible to be in the world but not of it, to reject the goals and claims of the dominant society while living as part of it, just as Paul did. Whether or not such rejection is sufficient to constitute faithfulness to the call to solidarity remains to be seen and decided upon in the larger community. But it certainly is possible for one to feel a stranger within one's own land.

The scope and seriousness of homelessness can be seen in the experiences of numerous exiles from Latin America, the Caribbean, Eastern Europe, Africa, and Asia who fill our land. Their plight is indescribably dreadful. The tragic circumstances of their homeland and their flight are often overshadowed by the pain of their situation in exile. They may have shelter, but they are without most of the roots that connected them to the soil out of which they grew. They are cut off and lonely, longing to return, but unable to. To characterize my feeling as "homelessness," in the light of their experiences, could seem to trivialize their tragedy. But to reject the dominant culture is precisely to find oneself in exile, and such rejection is part of the journey of some Euro-American males.

## Forms of Exile

There are two kinds of exile: imposed and chosen. Some forms of exile are imposed upon one either by political or natural circumstances. Israel was forced into exile by Babylon. Central American peasants, who only want the economic security that comes with owning a small plot of ground, find themselves blocked at every turn by political decisions, economic controls, and military force. Their option is either economic enslavement or exile. Thousands of young men fled our country for Canada during the Vietnam War because they were offered the option of the draft or conscientious objector status but were denied the possibility of resistance to the war by legally refusing to serve. Their options were prison or exile. Many who have raised their voices on behalf of human rights in South Africa, Latin America, the Soviet Union, and elsewhere have been hounded by the police or even by death squads. Their option has been either silence or exile. Major earthquakes have not only destroyed entire towns and communities but also have left those areas dangerous or uninhabitable. The residents have no choice but to leave or to wait for inevitable death. For many, the stakes are enormously high, and the options are clear—they cannot remain. This is imposed exile.

Sometimes the exile is not imposed but chosen because of a dream. Millions have come to our shores in the hope of finding streets of gold. For some, it is not the immediate situation in their homeland that has forced them to emigrate but a dream or a promise—whether economic, political, or personal. This was Abraham's experience. Abraham was not forced to become an exile. He was a man of considerable wealth, as evidenced by the servants and possessions he took with him when he left Ur of the Chaldees. Nor is there any indication that he was run out of the country or had to flee. Abraham became an exile by choice, because Yahweh invited him to share a vision of a greater vocation: "I will make of you a great nation, and I will bless you . . . and by you all the families of the earth shall be blessed" (Gen. 12:2–3).

Exile can be imposed or chosen; it can also be either physical or spiritual. We are most familiar with exile in its physical form. Our nation is filled with persons who have had to flee their homelands or who have chosen to come here to fulfill a dream. They have packed up family and goods and moved to a place that is unfamiliar in its language, customs, and systems.

While exile is usually thought of in geographical terms—physically leaving one country and moving or being moved to another—there is another kind of exile that is equally real. It is spiritual exile. William Stringfellow captured it well in the title of his book, *An Ethic for Christians and Other Aliens in a Strange Land.* He was writing to Christians in the United States who were living within their own country but experiencing a fundamental spiritual dislocation.

For those in spiritual exile the problem is one of being unable to give allegiance to the ruling values and arrangements of their culture or society. It is the exile experienced by those who watched the Ohio National Guard kill protesting students at Kent State University under the banner of law and order. It is the exile experienced by those who witnessed the politicians, the public, and the police as they saluted the flag but conspired to deny the civil rights of African Americans. It is the exile experienced by those who can no longer accept our nation's frenzied military build-up while millions of children attend underfunded schools, live in lead-contaminated housing, play in junk-filled yards, and live without a future. It is the exile experienced by those who discover that our nation's claims to international beneficence are mocked by our policies and military aid that support regimes employing death squads. It is possible to remain living within our own land, and yet not to feel ourselves to be "of" it.

To be in physical exile is to be unable to return, given the existing circumstances. To be in spiritual exile is to be unable to grant the allegiance that home deserves. It does not necessarily mean that one forgets about home or rejects home. In fact, the exiles' longing for home may be more deeply felt than the allegiance of those who enjoy its benefits.

Sometimes exile can be for immature reasons, such as the self-imposed exile of the prodigal son who rebelled against the values and arrangements of his father's house. So, in what might be termed adolescent rebellion, he turned his back on home and set out for another country to live life on terms that he considered better. It was only when he was reduced to a state of total degradation that he realized what the love and security of his home meant to him. Then he returned.

For some Euro-American males exile is more of an exercise in rebellion than a deep spiritual alienation. Many a privileged man has experimented with rebellion for a while, only to return to the privileges when the going got tough or he "grew up." In some circles rebellion is an accepted way for one to break from the control of one's parents, a form of sowing one's wild oats.

Some, however, choose exile for more substantive reasons. It is not simply rebellion and rejection of authority that drives them away, but the fundamental impossibility of living life according to the dictates of one's conscience and vision. In such a case, exile is not a temporary experiment but a painful way of life.

Several years ago I met a young man who was profoundly exiled, spiritually, from his own country. A small group had gathered in the office of U.S. Senator Frank Lautenberg to press for policy changes in relation to El Salvador and Nicaragua. The young man had been to Nicaragua recently and seen firsthand some of the devastating results of the Contras' torture, rapes, and killings. He spoke softly, at first, telling of his time in the Navy, his visit to Nicaragua, and finally of his growing alienation from his own country. Unable or unwilling to control himself any longer, his tears and rage mingled as he sought to find the words for his hatred and rejection of our government's policies and practices. He clenched his fist and sputtered, "Sometimes I just want to hit someone or something . . . I just want to stop us from doing what we're doing. . . . I don't know, I just can't stand it." He was an exile living within his own country.

Each of us needs a center, a home, a land that we can claim

as our own. We need to be able to love it and give allegiance to it and, at a certain level, trust ourselves to it. Home is where you neither need always to explain who you are nor to wonder who the others are. You can count on things; it isn't perfect, but there is enough you can count on to feel good about it. The exile, whether geographic or spiritual, has lost that.

People in spiritual exile haven't always known quite what to do to express the alienation they feel from their own society and culture because they have not had to leave physically. The symbols of spiritual exile aren't so readily apparent. Some have burned the flag, others have remained seated during the singing of the national anthem, and others have engaged in civil disobedience. The problem with some of these symbolic actions is that they have been easily interpreted as anti-patriotic. Nothing could be further from the truth.

The spiritual exile is, at core, a patriot. Whether forced or chosen, the exile lives with constant longing for her land. It is not simply a longing to return to the land, but a longing for its restoration. One of our greatest patriots was a spiritual exile who remained on our soil and fought until his death for the restoration of our nation to its true calling. Martin Luther King, Jr., lived the dilemma of an African American experiencing rejection within his own country while at the same time being a loyal citizen who could not and would not give up on his nation. Some have criticized King because he did not become a separatist or flee to Africa. They felt that by remaining to fight here he failed to understand the depth of the problem of racism and poverty. But King was not naive about the depth of the tragedy; he was no less an exile than James Baldwin, who left for France, or Eldridge Cleaver, who took refuge in Cuba. King understood that it is only the exile who can save our land. He did not use the word "exile", but in a strikingly similar way, he called upon "all men [*sic*] of good will to be maladjusted because it may well be that the salvation of our world lies in the hands of the maladjusted."[1]

The exile is one who is maladjusted, physically and/or spiritually, either because she has been forced out of her land or because she can no longer give allegiance to the values and arrangements that dominate it.

The power of a song we used to sing in church as I was growing up has new meaning for me. "This world is not my home, I'm just a-passin' through. My treasures are laid up, somewhere beyond the blue." While I no longer understand this in terms of an escape to some other-worldly sphere, I have found that the old gospel chorus is in touch with an important truth. We are strangers within our own land when the values and dreams we have are not being honored, when those with whom we live are no longer trustworthy, when social arrangements create alienation instead of oneness.

For many of us, exile or homelessness is self-imposed. No one told us that we had to cease being loyal to the existing values and arrangements. In fact, it is a constant struggle not to succumb. Everything conspires to convince us that we are crazy: crazy to see the evil we do, crazy not to join the crowd, crazy not to grab the brass ring and go for the gold, crazy to hold out for a vision that never can be fully realized. Even though we have chosen a certain kind of exile, we are still caught up in the arrangements and values we reject. There is no purity here, but, rather, a constant struggle within and without. At the core is a certain dislocation, a certain maladjustment, an exilic spirit.

This is the situation faced by all of us who discover that we can no longer give allegiance to what we formerly believed and from which we benefited. Choosing spiritual exile creates some strange dynamics for middle-class, straight, Euro-American males.

## Funny, You Don't Look Homeless

Euro-American males that choose spiritual exile are immediately suspect. Just as my friend could not at first believe my feeling of homelessness, most people who have had exile imposed upon them are quite naturally suspicious of those who have chosen exile, especially if they don't look like exiles. Objectively speaking, Euro-American males can go back to a privileged position anytime they choose, and that makes them suspect in the eyes of those who cannot. For some, their color, class, or gender prevents them from easily blending into the existing social arrangements. But not so for Euro-American males.

In the '60s there was a criticism made of persons who "borrowed" poverty, who opted to live the simple life but were able to return to affluence should they choose. Such persons frequently engendered suspicion. The same is true for people who choose spiritual exile. Whoever does not choose to serve the interests of the dominant society, but rather seeks to transform that culture, *is* outside the camp, regardless of appearances. Still, since some do slink back into the camp of the affluent with such ease, suspicion is appropriate.

Given human propensity for self-righteousness, it is not uncommon for each of us to think that our own form of exile, our own attempts at faithfulness, are the only authentic ones. Many of us have a tendency to think that ours is the only way to be in solidarity, to challenge the existing values and arrangements, to follow the claims of Christ. When I was growing up many in our church thought that there was a prescribed way to look like a Christian. Women were discouraged or prohibited from wearing make-up or slacks. Drinking, movies, dancing, and playing cards were likewise banned. Within that world in which the lines were clearly drawn, it was possible to know who was inside and who was outside. There are persons within the solidarity movement who exhibit the same mentality. There is only one way to be an exile. If you don't fit the description, you are not to be trusted.

I've often wondered about the suspicion the apostle Paul must have engendered by maintaining his Roman citizenship, and even using it to his advantage on occasion. Although it was his stated intention to use it for the sake of furthering the gospel, I wonder whether the early Christians who were not Roman citizens and who were persecuted by Rome resented his holding Roman citizenship. Did it make him suspect? He had converted from Saul to Paul. Could he not return to being Saul anytime he chose? The answer to the latter question is obviously yes, just as Jesus could have turned away from Jerusalem and the consequences he faced there. Anyone who is in spiritual exile is capable of selling out and resuming the former condition with all its benefits.

The recognition of this generic possibility of selling out does little to minimize the suspicion directed toward Euro-American men, given the history of white liberalism. Albert Memmi has written insightfully about the plight of the colonizer who recognizes the injustice of colonialization and wishes to "refuse" the system, but who, nonetheless, is unwilling to give up the benefits she or he enjoys.[2] "The colonizer who refuses" wants to have cake and eat it too, to have a clear conscience but to continue benefiting from the injustice. Anyone who is a "spiritual" exile and who looks the same as the dominant group can easily fall into that trap, so suspicion is warranted even though it is not always applicable.

There is no way for any of us to avoid suspicion. That is the reality of the solidarity movement. We would do well to save our energy by not being constantly surprised when we are suspected, not being constantly on the defensive, not being constantly hurt. Perhaps that is too simplistic. It still hurts, but at least we don't need to waste quite as much energy defending ourselves against the inevitable, and we can get on with the task at hand.

## "Sometimes I Feel Like a Motherless Child"

When you choose spiritual exile one of the things you don't anticipate is the ferocity of the loneliness. You have left behind those who were friends, and you have entered a new world in which you are suspect.

Certainly I have overstated the case somewhat. Spiritual exiles have continuing relationships with persons who are part of the homeland, part of the dominant culture. We live in their midst, we are related to them, they are part of our history. But it is not the same. The fullness of friendship is absent. Some of the most fundamental questions and longings are not shared or even understood. At the deepest level, we cannot pray with them. And certainly the exile's critique and rejection of the dominant values and social arrangements are not shared.

Without the normal activities and relationships that pass for friendships within Western culture, life can appear rather barren. Even though many of these relationships were superficial, there was an aura of camaraderie that covered up their shallowness. Constant partying and entertaining often passed for friendships. For Euro-American males the locker room often became a kind of home. If one only kept busy enough, there was seldom time to face the absence of any depth. Social connections took the place of a community of sharing.

When Euro-American males accept the emptiness of their own culture, there is nothing they want more than friendship and community. Because they have rejected the dominant culture, few who look like them will share their journey. So they look for friends among the oppressed. But because they are suspected by the communities of the oppressed, it is rare that they will find themselves accepted there either. They may be treated as a guest, with grace and hospitality, but they won't get to kick off their shoes and share at the most intimate levels. That comes only rarely and after a long time.

Many Euro-American males are terribly impatient. Those who have grown up as middle-class Euro-American males in the United States have often come to expect that almost everything can be accomplished immediately. They've come to think that with a little bit of pushing, a little cajoling, a little politicking, things can get done—today. Given this, it is extremely difficult to have to wait to be accepted or to make friends. The waiting period is a time of loneliness, compounded by impatience. And there is nothing they can do to speed up the time frame or to ensure the results.

This loneliness is compounded by the limited experience that many Euro-American males have in developing deep friendships. Western society is so individualistic that even when consciously seeking exile from it, one retains the automatic reflexes that work against community. These tendencies often create hindrances for others whose culture values community and friendship. Many Euro-American men experience this in their friendships with women. For those men who have been socialized to think of women as possessions for their individual pleasure, the possibility for genuine intimacy with women is blocked. One may be grateful that some women have seen beyond these limits, hung in there, and helped some men learn how to be a friend.

Spiritual exiles need to accept their loneliness. It is a time of wandering in the wilderness, of praying alone in the garden, of being tested in the desert. For someone used to being surrounded by people and activities, used to constant acceptance and affirmation, the loneliness feels strange. We do not like it. But it is part of the refining process by which our mettle is made stronger for the battle ahead.

## *"How Ya Gonna Keep 'Em Down on the Farm?"*

When you are brought up with privileges, no matter what kind, you begin to take them for granted. They are part of life. While the majority of professional Euro-American males lack any real control over the basic economic or political decisions, they nonetheless grow up believing that they belong, that they are among the privileged.

I remember my surprise when an African American colleague told me that she always went to the bathroom before leaving home or work because she knew that once she left, there would be no place available to her. I inquired why she didn't go to hotel or restaurant restrooms. It was my assumption that, in most cases, if she simply walked in as if she belonged, she would not be stopped. Her incredulity made me aware of just how much many of us take for granted.

People who have come to take privileges for granted and then choose spiritual exile are prone to waver. When you grow up with privileges—no matter how ill-gotten, no matter how skewed or limited—and decide to reject them, the temptation is to return to them.

When the children of Israel languished in the wilderness, eating monotonous meals of manna, uncertain about where they were going and when they would arrive, they began to murmur and to long for Egypt. Never mind that slavery went along with the leeks and garlic. They had tasted something and now missed it. As the song puts it, "How ya gonna keep 'em down on the farm, after they've seen Par-ee?" If even Egypt looked good to the children of Israel, what is to keep us from wanting to return to a life of privilege?

Most of us who have chosen a form of spiritual exile find ourselves tempted to return to a place of privilege that we can take for granted. We experience this in a number of ways. Many of us grew up thinking that we had the answers and were the ones who should be in charge. It is a slow and difficult process to come to believe that others have gifts that will collectively contribute to a given task. Even after affirming and adopting a more collegial manner, when things are not being done the way we would like, there is a temptation to try to take back control, to recover the very privilege that we've consciously rejected.

This wavering is similar to the dynamics of giving up smoking. The cigarettes may have been killing us and those around us. We know that we and everyone else are better off without them, but when things get tough we find ourselves reaching for a smoke. That's the way it is for the spiritual exile. There is nothing stopping us from returning to the privileges of our former homeland, except our resolve. And sometimes resolve isn't enough.

Others have recognized the inordinate burden and the high risk of trying to maintain resolve in the face of temptation and weakness, and they have discovered the necessity for public accountability. Those who give up smoking often find it necessary or important to have others with whom they share their struggle. Alcoholics Anonymous is built on this principle. So, too, is the church. At the heart of the Christian liturgy is the confession which offers us the opportunity to be publicly accountable. Public accountability cannot guarantee we will not waver, but it can help to call us to faithfulness.

## Look Who Thinks He's Nothing

A rabbi and cantor were preparing for the High Holy Days. As they stood together before the Torah each expressed contrition for his shortcomings. The rabbi beat his breast and exclaimed, "O God, I am nothing." The cantor bowed low and intoned, "O God, I, too, am nothing." At the back of the synagogue the custodian had been watching silently. Deeply moved, he came forward, threw himself on the floor and cried out, "O God, I, too, am nothing. I am the lowest of the low." Seeing this, the rabbi turned to the cantor and said with disdain, "So look who thinks he's nothing."

A lot of us revel in our guilt. We seem to think that it provides a basis for solidarity. For Euro-American males it is as if they hope to find acceptance from those whom they hurt—God, spouse, parents, African Americans, Hispanics, women—by acknowledging their own evil. There is a time for guilt, to be sure. There are actions we all take or do not take that do cause injury or set in motion negative effects. Then it is appropriate to acknowledge the guilt we bear. But guilt can become a way of life, and when it does it works against genuine solidarity.

Many Euro-American men who want to be in solidarity often succumb to the guilt trap. At some level it is the result of genuine remorse and sadness for the injustices that abound. For people who are empathic to the needs of the oppressed and, at the same time, benefit from injustices, there is a tendency to feel guilt for their complicity, even if they did not create the unjust situation. But often guilt goes far beyond that and seems more like a knee-jerk reaction. If something is wrong, it must be their fault. This results in an unhealthy relationship for all concerned. Just as some marriages involve a guilt-ridden partner and another who milks that guilt for all that can be gotten out of it, so, too, many attempts at solidarity are built upon sick guilt relationships. Many professional Euro-American male progressives have sought to build solidarity based upon their guilt. And, at the same time, some members of the oppressed community have been quick to collude with them, deriving a sense of power by demeaning and exercising control over those who feel guilty. Inappropriate guilt cannot build solidarity but only counter-dependency.

Inappropriate guilt is also counterproductive with peers. For example, it cuts progressive Euro-American males off from other middle-class Euro-Americans who have not yet come to understand the world in the same way. Many of them are fine people who love their family and friends, who support the church and charities, who work hard, who wish for a kinder and more just world, and who don't want to hurt anyone. But they do not understand how their way of life contributes to world poverty; they do not understand that racism benefits them and hurts people of color; they do not understand that patriarchy still has a stranglehold on women who "have come a long way." Rather than laying a guilt-trip by implication upon them, Euro-American males who are socially aware need to patiently take them on a journey of discovery.

Inappropriate guilt is not just a matter of individual behavior; it can be structured into the society. Affirmative action, an appropriate attempt to correct an historic evil, has been developed in such a way that it depends upon feelings of inappropriate guilt among working class Euro-American males. It is a legislative corrective that blames the wrong persons and fails to exact payment from whom it should. When a Euro-American man's job is threatened it is unrealistic to expect him to feel guilt for his racism or sexism and to accept the corrective of affirmative action that is being imposed. He feels that he did not create the situation; he has played by the rules of the game. He cannot see how he is guilty. And in some significant respects he is correct. The fact is that he is the scapegoat, the sacrificial lamb. It is the larger societal patterns, the history and structures of the economy and politics, and the power brokers that have created the situation. It is totally understandable that he would not feel guilt for taking a job from someone else when he needs the job in order to support his own family, and when all he did was to play according to the rules. Yet we expect him to knuckle under, and we criticize him when he fights for his job. We plead for fair play and try to play on his guilt. But guilt won't work. Only in the most removed fashion is he guilty, and to expect him to feel guilt only widens the gulf between him and those who are being offered the job in his place.

Do not misunderstand. I support affirmative action, but not as it is currently conducted. What we have now is the creation of a small group of sacrificial lambs who are made to pay for the sins of several hundred years. We have assigned guilt to a select few, and the wrong ones at that, but have not faced the larger issue of responsibility. Generally speaking, those whom we select for sacrifice are near the bottom of the totem pole. While it is true that all Euro-American males have at least indirectly benefited from the racism and sexism of our economy, those sacrificed on the altar of affirmative action are not the primary beneficiaries. They are lambs led to the slaughter unwillingly. The real beneficiaries continue to reap as before. The chief executive officers remain in their jobs. The children of the rich still are admitted to the schools of their choice.

Authentic affirmative action would address the problem of access to employment, advancement, education, and other opportunities by spreading the costs much more widely. The answer is to reallocate resources so as to provide jobs for all, education for all, an answer that will mean the end of excessive wealth and privilege for the few in control. We cannot have authentic affirmative action so long as we maintain the fundamental structures of power and privilege. All we will have are appointed scapegoats.

In forcing selected individuals to pay for the sins of our society, rather than creating a system of restitution that spreads the costs fairly, we are creating an enormous backlash that lays the groundwork for fascism, thus feeding the neo-Nazi, Ku Klux Klan, and Aryan supremacy groups that have been on the rise. We have substituted guilt for responsibility and sacrificial lambs for societal restitution. The consequence is predictable. This assignment of guilt will not produce solidarity but deeper divisions. Those who wallow in guilt will not be able to understand this dynamic. Their response will be to deepen the blame, expecting others to join in the litany of guilt. But inappropriate guilt will only widen the gap.

## Hey Bro', What's Happenin'?

Another common dynamic for Euro-American males who find themselves in spiritual exile is the tendency to become parasites. If they believe that the values and arrangements that form the basis for Western culture are bankrupt, where do they turn? Often they try to borrow another culture and identity.

Such men have, in effect, cut off the roots of their own identity. If they were brought up in a society that told them in so many ways that they were superior to women and people of color, and they rejected that identity, where do they turn for a new identity? If they were brought up in a culture that told them that feelings were not to be trusted, and they rejected that truncation, where do they turn for a more holistic model of life? If they were brought up in an environment that told them the only way to survive is to beat the competition and to exploit everything around them, and they rejected that way of being, where do they turn for new sources of behavior? If they cannot turn to the Euro-American male-dominated culture, then where can they turn?

It is at this point that so many Euro-American males have tried to borrow another culture. They have tried to be African American, talking jive or giving five, or to be like women, or to become Latino. This is quite understandable. Often an awakening to the bankruptcy of one's own culture has gone hand in hand with exposure to dimensions and experiences of other cultures. Many Euro-Americans were introduced to dance through the music and movement of African Americans. Maybe they didn't quite get it, but the "soul" that they discovered was compelling. Naturally, the temptation is great to try to become as African American as possible in order to absorb as much of this newfound richness as they can. But that doesn't work.

The particularity of another person's culture or race or gender is not something one can put on like a suit of clothes. It comes from birth and a lifetime of living. Learning a few phrases, mannerisms, behaviors, or moves may provide some basis for connection, but it is not the same as "becoming" the other. We can see this when it comes to learning a language. It is a rarity for a foreigner to learn to speak another language as a native. While we may master the mechanics and vocabulary, the intangibles of communications—gestures, facial expressions, inflections, tonality—continue to elude us. If learning a language is so difficult, how much more the learning of another culture's history, inner expectations, fears, hopes, and dreams. While people may learn from others, they cannot become them. This is true at the one-to-one level and at the broader cultural level.

Euro-Americans cannot melt easily into another culture. The differences give them away. In parts of Maine it is common for people who were born elsewhere, but who have lived there for most of their lives, still to be considered "from away." If it is difficult for someone from another part of New England to be accepted in Maine, how much more difficult must it be to find acceptance within the many cultures of the larger society where the differences are so much more pronounced.

Certainly it is possible to learn from others and to change substantially, but Euro-Americans need to be careful that they are not simply parasites, drawing all their vitality from another source and contributing nothing to it. Parasites pose a very real danger to the culture from which the vitality is being drawn. We've all seen the way advertising and political campaigns have crassly borrowed phrases, music, and dress modes from oppressed communities and used them for totally contrary purposes, at the same time cheapening and trivializing the power of the original expression. Even those who wish to go deeper, to get in touch with the soul of a culture that is not theirs, need to be careful that they do not diminish its power. I sometimes wonder if the Euro-American community's use of spirituals and the blues doesn't serve to diminish them. Do they become only entertainment in Euro-American hands? Perhaps this fear is unfounded; the power of the oppressed cultures may be sufficient to withstand this drawing from them. But I doubt any culture can remain healthy if the society around it is constantly draining it and giving nothing back.

What I am certain of is that treating other cultures in a parasitical way does significant damage to the one acting as parasite. Just as for any parasite, existence then becomes totally dependent upon an external source. Euro-Americans who become cultural parasites ignore whatever sources of life there may be within their own being, and in doing so these capacities atrophy. Whatever they fail to nourish out of their own sources will soon become useless. The consequence is that they will have nothing to offer.

This danger leads to a final consideration, the exploration of what there is within Western culture that is worth preserving and that can make a contribution to the struggle for liberation. Euro-Americans who wish to be in solidarity with oppressed people need to move beyond breast-beating and the denial of anything worthwhile within their own culture. At the same time they should not succumb to the hubris and arrogance that has so often accompanied their sense of worth. The task before them is to reclaim their own heritage in a way that avoids treating it as totally depraved but, at the same time, recognizes the radical nature of their fall. What is there for them to claim, to hone, to offer? Unless they can affirm something of their own, they will have nothing to offer as friends or allies.

# For Reflection

1.  A black preacher, addressing a group of mostly Euro-American men, said, "I feel sorry for the white male. He has no sense of identity. He has no cause. He belongs to no one but himself." Would you agree with this assessment?

2.  Do you experience strong bonds of kinship with others who are like you? How does your experience of kinship or loneliness compare with those whose race, gender, class, or sexual orientation is different from yours?

3.  Is spiritual homelessness or exile a new idea to you? Do you feel so profoundly estranged from the dominant culture that you consider yourself an exile?

4.  If you consider yourself a spiritual exile, do you struggle with the temptation to "return" to the dominant culture? Are there others to whom you feel accountable in this struggle?

5.  How would you define "patriotism"? How can a person be both a patriot and a spiritual exile? Have you ever participated in a symbolic protest, such as refusing to pledge allegiance to the flag? How do you feel about such actions?

6.  Make a list of the ways in which Euro-American males have profited from the exploitation of Native Americans, Hispanics, African Americans, women, and the poor. Be sure to consider education, job, economic advantages, the fruits of colonialism, land ownership, class/gender authority, and ecological abuses.

7.  As a Euro-American male, for how much of this exploitation do you feel personally responsible? How many advantages are you willing to surrender for the sake of

fairness and solidarity? Would it be possible for all people to live at the level you do?

8.   At many points in life we are profoundly influenced by the people around us. Have you ever tried to borrow a culture different from your own? What were the results? Can you think of examples when advertising and media have cheapened the ways of other cultures? Why do we sometimes fall into the opposite trap of unrealistically idealizing other cultures?

# For Further Discussion

1.   The Bible abounds with images and metaphors of spiritual exile. Consider Hebrews 11:8–16; John 17:11–19; Luke 9:57–58. What common threads do you find in these passages? How does this commonality speak to your experience? In what sense was Jesus an exile? Is it possible to be a Christian without being an exile?

2.   Is it possible to be in exile from selected aspects of the Western lifestyle? If you are a spiritual exile, what aspects of our culture have displaced you? To what areas of the culture do you still feel loyal?

3.   Who do you think suffers more: the physical or the spiritual exile? The forced or the self-imposed exile? Why?

4.   What is the difference between exile as rebellion and exile as spiritual alienation? How would you classify a conscientious objector? A person who fled to Canada during the Vietnam War? An executive who leaves his or her job to enroll in seminary? A wealthy person who moves into a ghetto? An heir who refuses an inheritance earned from military products?

5.   Why do you think God has given us the capacity to feel guilty? How can we distinguish between healthy and unhealthy guilt? What is the difference between corporate and individual guilt? Why is guilt unlikely to lead

toward solidarity? When does breast-beating become a cop-out?

6. Do you agree with the author's critique of affirmative action? Have you seen good results from affirmative action? Have you seen resentment and anger caused by affirmative action? How should affirmative action be practiced in order to bring about true reforms at all levels?

7. In what healthy ways have you been enriched by other cultures' food, language, family models, art and music, theology, holidays, or worship?

8. Are you relieved or distressed by the suggestion that Euro-American males ought to struggle primarily within their own communities? Why are they more likely to have an impact on their own institutions than would African Americans, women, or other groups?

# 6
# The Baby
# and the Bath Water

There is a tendency among those who are critical of their own culture and society to think that there is nothing within it to affirm. Or at least they often sound that way. There are two negative consequences of this tendency. The first is that such people alienate, rather than educate, those who are not already in agreement with that critique of their culture. The second is that persons who think there is nothing to affirm lose touch with those resources that could be useful in the cause of liberation.

Many of us have heard or have even borne the brunt of the vitriolic slogan, "America, love it or leave it." Undoubtedly some of those who respond in that manner will never be convinced that the critic or prophet sees anything good within her own country. There are people who think that criticism and love cannot coexist. Many more might be able to hear the criticism better if they also knew what it is that we affirm within our own heritage.

Martin Luther King, Jr., was masterful at confirming the positive elements of the United States experience—for example, the Constitution—while at the same time challenging the fundamental racism that has characterized our history. People could ignore or twist what he said, but only those who did not wish to hear could, in the long run, deny that he affirmed and loved his country in addition to criticizing it. In contrast to and partly because of the more total condemnation of the United States and Euro-American culture by Malcolm X, King's affirmations helped to win many to his cause.

There is more than just strategic value in not throwing out the baby with the bath water. There are often overlooked and critical resources present that need to be rediscovered. Persons from many of the oppressed groups within our society have begun the arduous search for their roots in order to discover positive aspects of their culture that have been buried. No longer willing to accept the oppressor's definition, they seek a new identity based upon a fuller understanding of their heritage. The same task faces Euro-American males. It is their responsibility to discover those aspects of their roots and of their current situation that provide a positive foundation from which to move forward in solidarity. No one is served by ignoring the positive elements of a culture simply because there is so much within it that must be rejected.

Implied in the metaphor of the baby and the bath water, of course, is the idea that the core of what is in the tub is worth keeping, and it is only that which has flowed in around it that is bad. The racist, imperialist, and patriarchal form of Western culture's development and expansion might lead us to question such an implication. But despite the evils associated with Western culture, there are positive aspects that should not be ignored. If we recognize the full range of results of the Enlightenment, the Reformation, and the French and American revolutions, which are central parts of U.S. heritage, we shall discover that there are some things worth saving as well as much to be discarded.

The Enlightenment, which stands at the heart of Western culture, has, among other things, provided us with the basis for modern science, and much of the impetus toward democracy. While it is fair to fault the excesses and perversions that have accompanied the rise of modern science, such as nuclear armaments and massive pollution, few of us would deny the positive gains achieved through the discovery of vaccines and antibiotics, or the inventions of electricity and the airplane.

While it is accurate to critique the French and American revolutions as benefiting the bourgeoisie rather than the impoverished, there can be no doubt that what was unleashed in those revolutions has had an impact upon freedom movements even to this day. Recent events in Eastern Europe and China underscore the power of the Western revolutionary legacy of freedom of expression, assembly, and the right to vote.

The Reformation's recovery of personal responsibility in matters of faith has shaped the very fabric of a "Protestant" United States. Even Roman Catholicism and Judaism, as practiced in this country, reflect the effects of this tradition. It is impossible to ignore the enormous strides in human freedom that are the result of the impetus provided by these aspects of Western heritage: freedom of speech, of travel, of communication, of assembly, of health, and so on. While it is our responsibility to critique the limits and perversions brought about by the powerful, who have utilized these gains for their own aggrandizement, it does us no good to ignore the significance of their benefits.

Sometimes it is difficult to see beyond the perversions and distortions, but we must. Generally speaking, progressives have been willing to separate the humane and helpful core from its perversions when it comes to things of the Left. We do that with Marxism. While the horrors of Stalinism and other forms of Communist party totalitarianism are sufficient to lead many persons to deny any validity to the thinking of Marx and Engels, most progressives have been able to see beyond the distortions to an essence they deem valuable.

Progressive Christians have also done the same with Christianity. The perversions of Constantine, the Crusades, the Inquisition, "Christian" Nazi Germany, or the Afrikaner church today in South Africa are enough to make any Christian with a modicum of sensitivity disown the faith. Over the centuries, countless horrors have been wrought in the name of

Christ. And yet progressive Christians do not turn their backs on Christianity, for they claim something more essential than the perversions.

It is reputed that Karl Marx once said, "I am not a Marxist." Jesus undoubtedly would have said, "I am not a Christian." Each would certainly reject the distortions and perversions carried out in his name. We who seek solidarity experience this truth, that even in the face of distortion and perversion there may be a salvageable core.

However, many progressive Euro-American males have been unwilling to find and affirm whatever truth and goodness might be present within their own Western heritage. Their reluctance is understandable, and yet they must undertake this task. It is important to face the distortions of reality inherent in one's culture and also to discover whatever truth still remains. It is important to recognize not only the limits but also the value and possibilities of one's culture, not simply to gain a hearing for prophetic criticism, but also for one's own sake. If we who are attempting to be in solidarity in the struggle for liberation fail to claim aspects of our heritage that could be helpful in the struggle, we do a disservice to all those with whom we wish to be in solidarity.

This has become apparent to me through my teaching at New York Theological Seminary. Three quarters of the seminary student body are people of color; almost half are women; many are truly poor or live in the midst of poverty. It came as no surprise to me that my criticism of racism, sexism, and classism was affirmed by these students. In that regard I was simply reaffirming many of their feelings and thoughts. What I did not expect was the affirmation I received for my contribution to the students' own thinking, personal development, and ministry. My identification of the evils of Western culture led me to think I had nothing positive to offer. Their response encouraged me to reassess my own gifts and the resources of my own background. I have been cautioned not to throw out the baby with the bath water.

What I share in this chapter is only a beginning. It is a beginning that needs to be expanded by others who are seeking to discern the gifts and the opportunities God has given them for the service of the oppressed. It is a beginning that needs to be critiqued by those with whom I seek to be in solidarity. It is certainly true that in longing to be part of a larger struggle, Euro-Americans can kid themselves about what they have to offer. If there is a temptation to think of themselves as nothing and to seek to borrow from others, there is also a temptation to succumb to the hubris and self-delusion that accompany privilege. With this in mind, I shall explore some of the opportunities and gifts Euro-American males in particular might offer in the service of solidarity for liberation.

Euro-American males are not the only ones who participate in the exercise of the following gifts. Many women and people of color have drunk at the well of Western culture and possess the very same capacities. Nor have all Euro-American males been the beneficiaries of the positive legacy of Western culture. There are millions of blue-collar workers who have simply been grist for grinding. But for those educated, middle-class males who have been significantly shaped by Western culture, it is time to assess what they can affirm so that they can bring more than longing, guilt, and emptiness to the quest for solidarity.

## *Seek and You Shall Find: The Gift of Expectation*

Two of the most popular books over the past several decades have been *The Power of Positive Thinking* and *How to Win Friends and Influence People.* [1] Each book draws upon the basic truth that if we expect positive results, positive results are more likely to happen than if we assume the worst; if we go after something we want, it is more likely to be achieved than if we simply sit back and wish for it; if we wish to be influential, there are certain things we can set out to do in order to succeed. Each of these claims or promises is quite true. The fact that each is only a partial truth does not take away from what these insights have to offer. The truth they contain has spawned an entire industry of self-help movements that "guarantee" success.

As one who has consistently criticized the myopia, smugness, elitism, and status quo orientation of the power-of-positive-thinking movement, I was completely caught off guard when my thoughts began to take this direction. This was not the kind of baby I expected to discover in the bath water. I think, however, that there is something in positive thinking that is worth affirming.

It is no mere coincidence that these two books were written by privileged Euro-American males. People who have experienced some degree of privilege often come to think of themselves as potentially successful, and it frequently works. But the success of these books has also been assured because positive thinking even works for some who have not been privileged.

In June of 1989 some of the faculty of New York Theological Seminary visited Korea. I had the opportunity to preach in a Presbyterian church there that had begun in 1948 with twenty-seven members who had fled from North Korea. Most of its early membership was made up of the persecuted and the impoverished. Today it is the largest Presbyterian church in the world with a membership of over sixty thousand. A Pentecostal church at which several others preached had twenty-five thousand members and had just raised over $8 million in three years for a new building. These are typical stories among the Korean churches. When you read the sermons and the literature produced by many of those churches, you discover a theology that is quite influenced by the "power of positive thinking." They dare to dream and to believe that the dream is possible.

The gift of expectation is a legacy of Western culture that we need to hold on to. It must be purged of its orientation toward growth in numbers rather than in quality, and it must be diverted from its role of serving the status quo to become a resource for fundamental transformation. The hubris that often accompanies such a stance needs to be eliminated. Too often people fail to recognize how significant a role existing privileges play in achieving success; conversely, they blame those who have given up hope for having brought the condition upon themselves. It is important to recognize that when you start out with boots, it is far easier to believe in the possibility of pulling yourself up by the bootstraps. Despite its inherent limitations and distortions, it is, nevertheless, a gift to believe that you can accomplish your dreams and longings.

There are times when a "can-do" attitude is quite helpful. Anyone who has played sports knows how critical a positive attitude is in winning. Community organizers have learned the importance of nurturing a sense of expectation among the people by achieving small victories and reminding them of the successes of others. When the odds against justice are so unfavorable, when victories are so sporadic, the spirit of a movement often weakens and sometimes disappears. Some of us have been given the spirit of expectation, and it would be foolhardy not to capitalize on this spirit. The question is how this spirit can be shared in solidarity without ignoring the tragedy of most people's lives and without feeling that one is somehow better or more filled with faith because of the expectation. Perhaps that spirit, if shared in humility, can be a gift that helps to revive halting steps and to stiffen backs bent by oppression.

## Reading the Signs of the Times: The Gift of Critical Thinking

One of the chief legacies of the Enlightenment is critical thinking, the ability to stand at a distance from something and analyze its components, its assumptions, its logic, its roots, and its implications. This is the principal foundation of modern science as it expressed itself in objectification, abstraction, and systematization. Without these abilities there would be none of the physical sciences as we know them today. Science is built upon more than just these abilities, of course, as studies in imagination and creativity have shown.[2] Abstract thinking existed long before the Enlightenment, but it came into its own with that watershed. The form of critical thinking that is the foundation of modern science is a gift of the Enlightenment.

Certainly there have been some unanticipated negative results from the utilization of this gift. Cornel West traces how the roots of racism were present in the objectification of the Western definitions of beauty. Without recognizing the implications of their selection and valuing, the philosophers who employed the so-called objective process lifted up the Greek form as the standard against which all other judgments of beauty were made. It was only a short step from there to the conclusion that people of African heritage were inferior.[3]

Those of us who have experienced the tyranny of objectification and abstraction have often sought other ways to understand reality. Poetry, mysticism, Eastern religions, the occult, and spiritualism have captured the imagination of many Westerners desirous of escaping the prison of objectivity and abstraction. This quest to move beyond the limits of abstract critical thinking is understandable and necessary, but it is insufficient in itself. The gift of critical thinking is enhanced by the presence of these less abstract capacities but cannot be replaced by them.

With the expanding epistemological base that has resulted from the rise of previously silenced voices, a critical reading of the signs of the times cannot be made by using only the intellectual gifts of the Enlightenment. The wisdom that comes from intuition, experience, meditation, and prayer is absolutely essential to discernment. I am often astounded by what I have missed in my analysis when confronted by the wisdom of an unschooled friend who simply "knows" some things I have never figured out. But this should not negate the importance of the intellectual task in the process of discernment. It is one of the gifts that, when combined with others, helps us to make faithful judgments about God's will.

If there is anything a Euro-American male is trained for in this culture, it is just such thinking (of course, many persons in addition to Euro-American males have been similarly trained). Even in the arts, a highly subjective arena, Euro-American males are trained to dissect the presentation as if it were a cadaver. All you have to do is listen to the movie critics (most of whom are Euro-American men) to understand something of this training.

For those who distrust critical thinking, it can pose a threat. An older African American woman enrolled in my class in eschatology. She had fought battles against racism, poverty, and sexism all her life. She knew what it was to be poor and discriminated against and to have doors constantly closed in her face. She also knew that the only way she had made it through these trials was because of God's faithfulness. She had heard of my expectation for critical thinking and announced on the first day of class, "I'm not going to let you take away my faith. I've come here double-glued."

For her, critical thinking meant giving up her faith. Despite the fact that I had met many others who shared her feelings, I was jolted by the forthrightness of her challenge and told her that the last thing in the world I wanted to do was to take away her faith. I explained that I was interested in helping her look at the ground on which she was standing and decide if it was rock or sand. It would be her decision whether to remain standing where she was. Fortunately her faith was strong enough, and she wanted the academic credits badly enough, to risk such a look. We persevered together, and she concluded the class with a faith that included a fuller understanding.

The ability to analyze critically is a gift of the Spirit that demands the same kind of discipline as prayer and meditation, the same kind of faithfulness as stewardship and administration, the same kind of passion as prophecy and evangelism. Just as the other gifts of the Spirit, its purpose is for the building up of the body. To the extent that Western culture and training have given this gift, it is the responsibility of persons with this gift to place it in the service of liberation. This can be one of their contributions to solidarity.

## Knock and It Shall Be Opened to You: The Gift of Access

Anyone can grow up to be president. But some are more likely to than others. Who you know, where you went to school, where you grew up, and how you look contribute greatly to getting your foot in the door of opportunity. This is common knowledge. "It is not what you know, it is who you know that counts." For some, a gentle tap on the door suffices.

Others must knock persistently. Jesus told a parable about a widow who repeatedly returned to plead with a judge for defense against her adversary. Such a situation would be analogous today to a woman seeking a restraining order against someone who was harassing or abusing her. According to the parable, the judge was known to be a man who did not fear even God, certainly not one who would give in to pressure. Yet, because of her persistence, he finally capitulated and ruled in her favor, lest "she wear me out" (Luke 18:1–8).

Imagine, however, if it were a friend of the judge who wanted help, another lawyer, perhaps. We are all too familiar with insider trading, political favors, and professional courtesy to hesitate very long in our imagining. Certainly the matter would have been expedited with haste. When you are one of the privileged, you don't have to waste a lot of energy knocking on the door.

It isn't fair, but that's the way it is. Because things work this way, many Euro-American males, especially professionals, have access to opportunities that others may never gain or may gain only after exorbitant expenditure of energy.

Earlier I mentioned the apostle Paul's use of his Roman citizenship. He certainly used it to further the cause of the gospel: gaining a hearing, dealing with the legal processes, and exercising the freedom to travel. Such a gift is not without its dangers, however. In fact, it may be precisely because of his privileges as a Roman citizen that he was willing to take the conservative stance he did with respect to the Roman government.

In Romans 13, Paul admonishes the church in Rome to be subject to the authorities, who, he said, had been ordained by

God. Christians have used this text over and over to quiet the voices of rebellion and resistance, insisting that anything less than unquestioning obedience to one's government is against God's will. Such a conclusion is thoroughly wrong when taken in the context of the full canon of scripture. From beginning to end the Bible teaches us that there is a higher authority to which we are accountable, namely, the authority of God; and when these two authorities, God and government, conflict, we are called upon to follow God's will. Within Paul's other writings it is clear that our basic allegiance is to God, not Rome. To account for this particular admonition of Paul, many biblical scholars have suggested that Paul believed that the return of Christ was imminent and the only important task was to proclaim the gospel. Since Roman civilization provided roads and protection for travel and communication, perhaps Paul thought Christians should not focus their energy fighting the government but instead use its services to spread the gospel. The issue of Rome's oppression was of secondary importance.

One of the dangers of access to privileges is that one can lose perspective. Perhaps Paul did. One of the temptations when one has such access is to extol silence, restraint, and acquiescence for the sake of what are considered more important goals. Such praise for passivity needs to be tempered by the cries of the people, and those who have some access to power should never underestimate the temptation to acquiesce to the injustices that continue to provide them with privileges.

Despite this danger, access to power is critical, and those who have it may use it for the sake of liberation. The Book of Genesis tells us about Jacob's son Joseph, who was sold into slavery in Egypt by his brothers. Through intelligence, attractiveness, and cleverness, he became a successful man and eventually rose to the position of governor. When there was a famine in the region, Egypt was prepared for it by virtue of Joseph's foresight and planning, the result of God's warning through dreams. The pharaoh used his food supply as a way to enslave all those who came to him for help. Among those starving from the famine were the children of Israel. When Joseph's father and brothers came to ask for help, they were not enslaved as were the others but, rather, were given places of responsibility and freedom. Their freedom was the direct result of Joseph's position in Egypt. He had access to the resources of the culture and was able to make them available to his family.

A lot of us have access. Many of us know people of some wealth. We may not know the enormously wealthy personally, but we know people who have money or who themselves have access to money: corporate managers, foundation personnel, government officials. Many of us have connections with decision makers or can make those connections. The truly marginal seldom get to sit with a senator or a mayor, with a corporation CEO or a foundation head, but many of the educated middle class can do that if we so decide.

Exercising the gift of access is a tricky business, and it is not for everyone. If we start to look or sound too much like the marginal rather than those with access, we soon get cut off. Daniel Berrigan no longer has the kind of access he once enjoyed as a respected priest. His numerous acts of civil disobedience and imprisonments have caused him to be viewed as an outsider. On the other hand, if we get too caught up in the culture to which we have access, it is easy to lose our perspective, to sell our soul. We all know prophets who have become members of the court. To exercise the gift of access we must be, as Jesus said, "wise as serpents and innocent as doves" (Matt. 10:16).

Those of us who can go almost anywhere we choose by virtue of our color, class, and gender have been afforded the gift of access. Most people see that as a ticket to their personal success. We who are committed to liberation and wish to be in solidarity should not turn our backs on this opportunity but seek ways to use our access for the sake of the struggle.

## *Living Between Cultures: The Gift of Freedom*

Earlier I spoke of the sense of spiritual homelessness many Euro-American males experience and the consequent loneliness and temptation to live off someone else's culture. But there is another side to this situation: exile can also be a gift. Those who stand between cultures can be free to allow the future to be open. If they are free to accept their condition as a gift rather than as a problem, they may be able to utilize this condition as a resource for liberation.

Perhaps to say that such exiles live between cultures is imprecise, more an image than a totally logical statement, since it is impossible to live without a culture. But it is an image that expresses my experience.

Our relationship to culture involves a choice. It is possible to decide what culture(s) will shape our lives and how it is to shape us. Culture is like sexuality. It is not possible to escape it, but it is possible to make decisions with respect to its influence and expression. The Roman Catholic Church understands this quite well. They have a requirement of celibacy for ordination to the priesthood. I am opposed to such a mandated restriction but support the personal choice of celibacy that many have made for the sake of their mission. The witness of many celibates, whether priests or not, is that they are free to address their fullest energies to the task before them. The point is that celibates do not cease to be sexual; rather, they have made a choice about their sexuality. Men and women decide to express their sexuality in certain ways and therefore to be influenced by it in certain ways.

The same principle applies with respect to one's relationship to culture. While it is not possible to be without a culture, as H. Richard Niebuhr has pointed out,[4] it is possible to make decisions with respect to culture: to accept the dominant one, to live in tension with it, to adopt an alternative culture, to seek to transform the dominant culture, or, some would add, to seek its overthrow.

When you are born into a culture and adopt it automatically and uncritically, whether it is the dominant culture or an oppressed culture, it is difficult to conceive of something different. The majority of the world's population relates to its culture in this manner. This is what might be called the "traditionalist's" stance. This is true not only of Third World peasant cultures, but also of subcultures within the United States. Residents of small towns and southern rural African American communities, Native Americans, and many first-generation immigrants inherit a traditionalist approach to culture in which what is received from the past more or less sets the limits for the future. For them, culture is to be accepted. Most Euro-Americans are also traditionalists with respect to the dominant culture.

On the other hand, people who have understood that no existing culture is adequate to express the vision to which they've been called are free to seek a new culture, to participate in the creation of a new culture. Culture is a human creation. All of us have the choice either to accept someone else's creation or to recreate one for our own time and place.

What lies ahead for human history need not be limited by the past but can be a new creation. And new creations emerge out of the chaos. Chaos is the womb of creation. Only those who recognize the chaos are free to seek a genuinely new creation, but there is nothing automatic about this freedom for a new future. It is possible to recognize the chaos and try to hold on for dear life, hoping that the inherited culture is sufficient to restore normality. That is the option of the so-called realists. They are not ignorant of the chaos. They simply think that it can be handled by what exists. They are nothing other than traditionalists dressed in contemporary clothing, believing that the dominant culture is sufficient. They are not freed to have a new vision because they are still at home in the culture.

The one who is willing to live between the times experiences a freedom that can contribute to the creation of a new culture. We see this in the arts. The creative artist is free from the normal constraints that circumscribe the dominant culture, free to imagine what has not yet been created. This is a freedom to hear what has only been whispered, see what has only been an apparition, feel what has only been a twinge. In painting or writing or dancing to these whispers, apparitions, and twinges, the artist stands in resistance to the larger culture and offers it new possibilities for self-understanding and organization.

We see this also in politics. The poetic confession of Martin Niemöller, a German pastor who lived through the rise of Hitler's regime, reveals the mind of a man finally converted to living between the cultures, no longer captive to the dominant one. Too late he came to understand that to create resistance and opt for the new requires an enormous act of the imagination, an imagination that understands that even though the threat to oneself may not be immediate, it is nonetheless inevitable. His words describing his reaction to the Nazi regime underscore the importance of being set free from the limits of a culture: "First they came for the Jews. I was silent. I was not a Jew. Then they came for the Communists. I was silent. I was not a Communist. Then they came for the trade unionists. I was silent. I was not a trade unionist. Then they came for me. There was no one left to speak for me."[5]

None of us stands totally free from our heritage. We may, however, find ourselves in tension with it, ill at ease, not at home. For those who experience homelessness, no culture— neither the inherited one nor those countercultures or subcultures around them—constitutes a secure place to rest. Because of this, we have the opportunity to ask questions, dream dreams, and look for new options. This is not a denial of culture and of the past but a recognition that the elements must be put together in a new way. It is an invitation for the act of imagination. Persons between cultures are not the only ones who can and should do this. But they are among those who should, because in living between cultures they have been granted the freedom to dream.

## Problem Solving: The Gift of Achievement

One of the most difficult reflexes for me to control is trying to fix things when people come to me with a problem. In fact, the very use of the word "problem" indicates what I'm struggling with. Learning to be present, to listen, and to nurture someone without always coming up with an answer runs against the grain for me. It is a struggle for many Euro-American males to overcome a problem-solving orientation, for this is a fundamental part of their legacy. But perhaps we need to distinguish between a problem-solving orientation and a problem-solving capacity.

Problem-solving is a part of the Western male legacy that can be placed in the service of liberation. It is partially born out of the expectation of success, but its roots run even deeper. There is a fundamental assumption behind the problem-solving mode that things do not have to remain as they are. Problem-solving grows out of a rejection of fatalism.

Many of the world's people live with fatalism. It is their assumption that their lot in life is ordained by God, in the stars, a matter of fate, or endemic to their own limits and failures as a person. In all cases, nothing fundamentally different is to be expected. This is not only true for the more "primitive" people who come from traditional cultures, but it is also prevalent among many within the United States. People feel that there is nothing to be done about government, business, the role of women, the poor on welfare, and so on. Each situation or group is as it is because of fate.

Others see situations as problems to be solved; that is, as opportunities. Much of our contemporary Western technology is the result of a problem-solving approach to life. If there is a task to be done, a mountain to be moved, a limit to be overcome, we turn our energies to the problem until we find a solution. The result has been an exponential growth in technological achievement that has contributed greatly to the quality of life for a good many people. To be sure, the majority of the world's population has gained little as yet, but, for the most part, the fault does not lie in the inventions or discoveries themselves. There is little in much of the technology to prevent gains in food production from eliminating world hunger. The failure to do so is a political-economic problem. There is nothing in the technology that prevents television from enhancing learning and worldwide communication.

Its failure to do so in the manner of which it is capable is a political-economic problem. Modern technology can be used to enhance all of the tasks of life, including the process of liberation. Technology is the result of a problem-solving capacity.

There is a serious danger of shallowness in the problem-solving approach, however, when it becomes an orientation to all of life. When a young mother of three children develops terminal cancer, it is not a "problem" but a tragedy. One of the most serious failures of modern medicine is the tendency of too many practitioners to treat sickness as a "problem" and not to recognize the fuller aspects of the person and situation. Holistic health care has flourished in this country as a corrective to this limitation. It is no coincidence that so much of the holistic approach to healing has come from women (e.g., midwifery), the Orient (e.g., the use of herbs), and the Third World (e.g., spiritism). Medicine as practiced in the West is essentially "a masculine, militaristic technology," as Joe Holland said to me in conversation.[6] It is "cut, burn, and poison." Problem-solvers don't do well with tragedy. It is at this point that the "masculine" limits become clear.

Despite these limits, the problem-solving capacity can be a gift. We need people to work on solving the problem of cancer so that the next young mother can be cured. Our responsibility is not to turn our backs on our technological, problem-solving legacy but to recognize its limits and seek to place it at the service of a larger community that can utilize it and complement it for the sake of liberation.

## "God Helping Me, I Can Do No Other": The Gift of Personal Responsibility

When Martin Luther stood before his accusers and was ordered to recant or be excommunicated, he refused to deny his beliefs. His reply of defiance stands till this day as an example of the individual standing against the crowd. This legacy of individuality, as expressed in the Reformation and elevated to grand heights in the Enlightenment, is at the heart of Western culture.

Unfortunately, it is a legacy whose perversion has contributed greatly to our divisions. Many of us have confused the exercise of personal responsibility with individualism, the myth of the isolated individual. There is no such entity as an isolated individual, and those who have tried to live the myth have experienced a deep loneliness and sense of alienation. Philip Slater has documented the larger collective costs of U.S. individualism as a nation built on the assumption that its people could keep moving on, leaving places and things and other people behind.[7] Criticism of U.S. individualism abounds in much of the sociological literature.[8]

There is no doubt that we have lost most of the communal sense and the communal skills that built ancient societies. Some pockets of the older life-style still are present within our nation, but the loss has been pervasive. The loss of the extended family, the decrease in a sense of public responsibility, the rise of privatized versus corporate religion, and the cult of the individual all underscore the conquest of individualism and the defeat of the communal.

There is also no doubt that we need to recover the reality of our communal interconnectedness, of our being one body, as well as the skills to build that body. The perversion of individualism and the loss of the communal do not deny the importance of personal responsibility. One of the great legacies of Western culture is the emphasis upon the rights of persons. This has translated into human rights and civil rights that most of us would affirm wholeheartedly. The right to vote, to speak freely, to travel without restriction, to choose one's partner are all rights that most Americans take for granted.

These rights that are associated with liberalism have profoundly shaped the character of Western culture. Despite their limits and problems, we do well to hold them dear. It is true that civil rights and human rights are not a substitute for economic justice. Just because you are allowed to sit at the same lunch counter does not ensure that you can afford the lunch. What liberals in the United States have consistently failed to understand is that political rights are only half the equation. Until we devise an economic system in which all people have certain basic economic rights and protection, we do not have true democracy. Real democracy includes both political and economic rights.

Our deficiency, however, is not cause to reject the importance of what rights we do have. There is an appropriateness to the focus on the person that must be maintained. This is the lesson of Eastern Europe and even China. They need not opt for a Western-style individualism to recover the truth of persons in community. It must be possible to affirm both. God comes to both the nation, Israel, for example, and specific persons, such as Isaiah in the temple and Moses in the wilderness. As a nation, Israel is called to responsibility for each person: widows, orphans, and children. As children of the covenant, all people are individually called to responsibility for the nation. In the flow between community and person lies wholeness.

In order for that interrelationship between community and person to exist, we must have both dimensions. Those of us whose heritage is excruciatingly individualistic need the chastening and challenge that come from the communities of the oppressed. When so reshaped, the individualism that has caused us to "look out for number one" can be transformed into an understanding of personal responsibility that is unwilling to bow the knee to the dominance of the crowd or the system.

The forces that led to Martin Luther's struggle with the Roman Catholic Church are still with us within the society and within the church. Today we are witnessing a battle within Roman Catholicism between a church hierarchy that understands community in terms of subservience and persons within the church who are trying to expand the community to allow for dissent and personal expression of the faith. Roman Catholicism has tended to submerse the person for the sake of the system, and the challenges to that church today are a direct result of the Western legacy of personal responsibility.

The problem goes far beyond the Roman Catholic Church, of course. Government is unresponsive, the economy is on a track in which the gap between rich and poor grows ever larger, the power of the traditional to hold sway seems impregnable, and the obstacles to liberation seem insurmountable. We will only prevail if we stand together, but we will only stand together when each of us is willing not to bow the knee to Baal, when each of us is willing to acknowledge our personal responsibility. Personal responsibility, when affirmed in community, can be a gift.

To write this chapter has not been easy. It is difficult to ferret out the wheat from the chaff. At the end of the day, that is God's business. I may be just plain wrong in my choice of what aspects of a Western heritage are worth keeping, and I certainly don't understand all of what I've begun here. Nor is this an attempt at a complete confession of either limits or gifts. It is difficult to publicly affirm gifts when their perversion has been so injurious to so many. It may be that the oppressed with whom I seek solidarity will see such an attempt as only self-serving. But just as this work emerged from a compulsion to seek our unity in Christ, so too it has demanded an attempt at honest appraisal. Its authenticity and helpfulness will be determined by others.

What I conclude is that all gifts are a form of power. The life-and-death question is: For what purpose is this power? Euro-American male culture has extended its own power through the self-serving use of its gifts rather than through serving others. Its technology has been used to expand empires and control the world, its intelligence to dictate orthodoxy, its access to ensure privilege, its self-confidence to suppress others, its sense of the person to secure a private world. When gifts are used for self-aggrandizement and for power over others, they become another source of division in an already fragmented world.

These very same gifts can be understood as the gifts of the Holy Spirit. When we understand that our capacities are the power of God in us, then we are freed to offer who we are and what we have for the sake of the whole creation. We do not need to wallow in self-pity and worthlessness. We can be free to take the risk of solidarity, to offer who we are and what we have for the sake of liberation. We can be free to say with Ruth, to all the oppressed who seek liberation, "Your people shall be my people and your God, my God."

# For Reflection

1.  Do you agree that Jesus would deny being a "Christian"? Why or why not? What aspects of Christian practice have been embarrassing to you? Why do sincere people cling to Christianity in spite of its historical failings?
2.  Do you have the gift of expectation? Can you recall an occasion when a positive attitude helped you succeed? What are the dangers inherent in a "gospel of success"?
3.  Why are so many people in the world still hungry and sick in spite of incredible scientific advances? Why do technological "solutions" so often cause additional problems?
4.  Have you ever used your gift of access to help someone else?
5.  Have you had experiences supporting the idea that modern medicine is "cut, burn, and poison"? What is holistic medicine? How can each approach learn from the other?
6.  How has an individualistic pioneer heritage shaped this country? What good things have we inherited from our pioneering forebears? What liabilities? How do other nations differ from the United States in this respect?
7.  As a Euro-American male, how would you answer a Hispanic woman who accused you of presumption in listing your culture's gifts?
8.  Can you personally affirm the gifts discussed in this chapter? Do you have other distinctive gifts which should be used for the common good? Are these gifts

that are shared by Euro-American males? Can you think of other gifts that ought to be offered in the service of solidarity?

# For Further Discussion

1.  Have you encountered people who seem to see nothing good in the prevailing culture? Do you ever feel that way about your culture? What problems arise from that attitude? Are liberals more generous in evaluating leftist governments than in appraising their own? How do you explain this?

2.  In what way does the Euro-American heritage and identity include the Enlightenment, the Reformation, and the French and American revolutions? What have those movements contributed to the modern world? What negative aspects have they introduced or enhanced?

3.  How does love temper criticism? With a partner, play the role of: a) an elder who must tell a beloved minister that his sermons have become repetitious; b) a woman who must confront her sister's overeating; c) an adult child who insists that an aging parent must give up his or her driver's license. How do you express criticism to people you care about?

4.  What conditions engender despair and fatalism among poor and oppressed people? How does the expectation of failure manifest itself among exploited people? How can we share the gift of expectation with people mired in futility?

5.  What is the gift of critical thinking and how has it grown from the Enlightenment? What are the values of critical thinking? The dangers and weaknesses? What other kinds of wisdom might be yoked to intellectual discernment?

6.  What gifts of access were available to Jesus because he was a healthy Jewish male? How did he use those gifts?

What doors are open to you simply because of your gender, color, and place in society?

7.  The earliest Christians believed that they lived "between the times," poised between the dying world order and the coming reign of Christ. How did this conviction liberate the early church? As Christians, are we liberated by our position "between cultures"? What choices can we make regarding the present culture? Regarding the future?

8.  What is the difference between a problem-solving capacity and a problem-solving orientation? How can we practice one without succumbing to the other?

9.  How does personal responsibility differ from individualism? How can personal responsibility strengthen community? How can community inform personal responsibility?

10. How would the gifts we have discussed be useful in organizing a neighborhood ministry? Protesting the action of a school board? Procuring financing for an innovative business? Comforting a mother whose child died for lack of medical treatment? Working for inclusive leadership in a congregation?

11. How can we distinguish between arrogance and a healthy pride in our gifts? Is it all right for Euro-American males to feel good about who they are? Why are they often reluctant to admit their gifts and strengths? How does the celebration of our own God-given abilities and resources empower us for the cause of solidarity?

# Notes

## Chapter One

1. Martin Buber, *I and Thou,* ed. Walter Kaufman (New York: Charles Scribner's Sons, 1970), p. 69.

2. For an analysis of the consistent failure of the Left within the United States to deal adequately with the issue of racism, see Robert L. Allen, *Reluctant Reformers: Racism and Social Movements in the United States* (Garden City, N.Y.: Anchor Press, 1975).

3. See Max Weber on the "Routinization of Charisma" in *Economy and Society,* vol. 1, ed. Gunther Ross (Berkeley, Calif.: University of California Press, 1978), p. 241ff.

4. For a treatment of this history see Gayraud S. Wilmore's "Identity and Integration: Black Presbyterians and Their Allies in the Twentieth Century" in *The Presbyterian Predicament: Six Perspectives,* eds. Milton J. Coalter, John M. Mulder, and Louis B. Weeks (Louisville: Westminster/John Knox Press, 1990).

5. James R. Kelly, "Spirals Not Cycles: Toward an Analytic Approach to the Sources and Stages of Ecumenism," *Review of Religious Research,* vol. 32, no. 1 (September 1990): 5–15.

6. Jacques Ellul, *Jesus and Marx: From Gospel to Ideology* (Grand Rapids: Wm. B. Eerdmans Publishing Co., 1981).

7. Melanie A. May, *Bonds of Unity: Women, Theology, and the Worldwide Church* (Atlanta: Scholars Press, 1989).

8. *The Kairos Document,* rev. 2nd ed. (Grand Rapids: Wm. B. Eerdmans Publishing Co., 1986), p. 11.

9. Juan Luis Segundo, *The Liberation of Theology* (Maryknoll, N. Y.: Orbis Books, 1976).

10. For an excellent overview and analysis of this school of thought, see George Ritzer, *Sociological Theory,* 2nd ed. (New York: Alfred A. Knopf, 1988), pp. 201–225.

11. For a fuller treatment of this difference, see Russell Pregeant, *Mystery Without Magic* (Bloomington, Ind.: Meyer Stone Books, 1988).

## Chapter Two

1. Elisabeth Schüssler Fiorenza, *In Memory of Her* (New York: Crossroad, 1986).

2. See Kuhn's discussion in *The Structure of Scientific Revolutions* (Chicago: University of Chicago Press, 1962) and my summary comments in T. Richard Snyder, *Once You Were No People* (New York: Crossroad, 1988), pp. 59, 60.

3. Fiorenza, *In Memory of Her,* pp. 48–52.

## Chapter Three

1. This approach has historical precedent within F. D. Maurice's treatment of the relationship between the mystical body of Christ and the option for socialism, which he developed in nineteenth-century England; in the basic thrust of the Life and Work movement of the early twentieth century; and in Latin American liberation theology. Gustavo Gutierrez's foundational work, *A Theology of Liberation* (Maryknoll, N.Y.: Orbis Books, 1973), treats the relationship between unity, Christian solidarity, and class struggle.

2. Gutierrez, *A Theology of Liberation,* p. 278.

3. James Cone, *God of the Oppressed* (New York: Seabury, 1975), p. 238.

4. Gutierrez, *A Theology of Liberation,* pp. 56ff.

5. See, e.g., Gustavo Gutierrez, *We Drink from Our Own Wells: The Spiritual Journey of a People* (Maryknoll, N.Y.: Orbis Books, 1984); James Cone, *The Spirituals and the Blues* (Westport, Conn.: Greenwood Press, 1980); and Robert McAfee Brown, *Spirituality and Liberation: The Great Fallacy* (Philadelphia: Westminster Press, 1988).

6. Paul Tillich, *Love, Power, and Justice* (New York: Oxford University Press, 1960), p. 8.

7. Thomas Kuhn, *The Structure of Scientific Revolutions* (Chicago: University of Chicago Press, 1962).

8. Beverly W. Harrison and Carol Robb, eds., *Making the Connections* (Boston: Beacon Press, 1965), pp. 231ff.

9. Sallie McFague, *Models of God: Theology for an Ecological Nuclear Age* (Minneapolis: Augsburg Fortress Press, 1987), ch. 6.

10. Martin Buber, *I and Thou,* ed. Walter Kaufman (New York: Charles Scribner's Sons, 1970).

11. InterSeminary Theological Education for Ministry (ISTEM) was a program of General, Union, New York, and Auburn seminaries and Yale Divinity School and was based in New York City.

## Chapter Four

1. Snyder, *Once You Were No People,* p. 46.

2. Several recent examples of this more integrated analysis of the structures of evil are James Cone, *For My People* (Maryknoll, N.Y.: Orbis Books, 1984) and Sharon Welch, *A Feminist's Ethic of Risk* (Minneapolis: Augsburg Fortress Press, 1989).

3. Snyder, *Once You Were No People,* pp. 70ff.

4. For a summary of this dynamic see chapter 7 in Jacquelyn Grant, *White Women's Christ and Black Women's Jesus* (Atlanta: Scholars Press, 1989).

## Chapter Five

1. From "The American Dream," a commencement address given at Lincoln University, June 6, 1961, in *A Testament of Hope: The Essential Writings of Martin Luther King, Jr.,* ed. James M. Washington (San Francisco: Harper and Row, 1986), p. 216.

2. Albert Memmi, *The Colonizer and the Colonized,* trans. Howard Greenfield (Boston: Beacon Press, 1991).

## Chapter Six

1. Norman Vincent Peale, *The Power of Positive Thinking,* 35th anniversary edition, rev. ed. (Englewood Cliffs, N.J.: Prentice-Hall, 1987) and

Dale Carnegie and Dorothy Carnegie, *How to Win Friends and Influence People,* rev. ed. (New York: Simon and Schuster, 1981).

2. Harold Rugg, *Imagination* (New York: Harper and Row, 1963).

3. Cornel West, *Prophesy Deliverance! An Afro-American Revolutionary Christianity* (Philadelphia: Westminster Press, 1982).

4. H. Richard Niebuhr, *Christ and Culture* (New York: Harper and Row, 1956).

5. As quoted in his obituary, *London Times,* 8 March 1984.

6. Joe Holland was formerly codirector of The Center for Concern, Washington, D.C., and is currently director of the Warwick Institute, South Orange, N.J., and visiting professor at St. Thomas University, Miami, Fla.

7. Philip Slater, *The Pursuit of Loneliness: American Culture at the Breaking Point,* rev. ed. (Boston: Beacon Press, 1976).

8. See, e.g., Robert N. Bellah et al., *Habits of the Heart: Individualism and Commitment in American Life* (New York: Harper and Row, 1986).